Ready
steady...Can!

KATH KELLY

Ready Steady... Can!

Ready steady...
CAN!
100 days, 120 canny recipes...
and that's just for openers!

Kath Kelly's off on another challenge: a test of resourcefulness and creativity on the remote island of Barra. She brings to this book the experience of years of tight-budget living and hitch-hiking around the world, tasting many cultures' cuisines. Fast-forward to her new life in the furthest, wildest corner of Britain, and to these intriguing experiments in her less than well-equipped Hebridean kitchen. Try her vegetarian recipes for Whisking Galore Chickpea Pavlova, Witch's Earwax Hallowe'en Claggum, Alright Jackfruit Fajitas, Sweet Surprise Pea Cake or Pan Can Farinata. Among the startling successes and the odd philosophically-faced flop, Kath lives, learns and laughs her way through a hundred days with a can-opener. This true story offers a peek through the window into her quirky world, facing the everyday demands of a life less ordinary and coming back for more!

Contents

Thank you to our friends and neighbours, who kindly acted as guinea-pigs over these one hundred days. They came, they chewed and they commented. They were generous with their time and helpful with suggestions. They offered constructive criticism, recipe ideas and gifts of peculiar cans.

Thanks most of all to Bruce, who gamely put up with my endeavours while letting me have the kitchen to myself. He can put a decent dinner together himself – when he gets a chance! Thank you, Bruce, for saying nice things about the foods you liked and being honest about the ones you didn't.

Other books by Kath Kelly (all available at Amazon.co.uk in Kindle format or paperback)

How I Lived a Year on Just a Pound a Day

Square Meals for Tough Times

Doing the Right Thing

Barra Visitors' Thrifty Fifty

A Ship of Fools

Reflections on the Road

Thumbing Through: Hitch-hiking Tales from my Diaries

RECIPES BY DAY

Day 71: **CAN EMPANADAS**
Day 72: **SMASHIN' MASH-UP TRAYBAKE**
Day 73: **BUNNY CHOW CAN-STYLE**
Day 74: **CIDER APPLE CAN LOAF**
Day 75: **SLAW UNTO ITSELF**
CANNED MEALIE BREAD
Day 76: **CAN-NOODLING AT LUNCHTIME**
Day 77: **MEXI-CAN ENCHILADAS**
FLOUR TORTILLAS
Day 78: **TIN TOM FRUIT TART**
Day 79: **PAN CAN FARINATA**
Day 80: **LAZY LATTICE PIE**
PASTRY NIBNOBS
Day 81: **SWEET AND SOUR CHOPSTICK KEBABS**
Day 82: **BORLOTTI BEAN CAKE**
Day 83: **STUFFED LYCHEES**
Day 84: **EXCEEDINGLY GOOD FAKES**
PINEAPPLE CHEESE PIE
Day 85: **BESIDE A CIDER STROGANOFF**
Day 86: **EASY TIN TIRAMISU**
Day 87: **MICRO-DUMPLING TINNED SOUP TEASE-OUT**
Day 88: **UPMA**
Day 89: **PEAS PLEASE ME SOUP**
Day 90: **CAN O' WORMS HALLOWE'EN CUPCAKES**
Day 91: **STICKY SAUSAGE SPAGHETTI**
Day 92: **CRUMBLE GRATIN TOPPING FOR SOUP OR STEW**
Day 93: **TIN TAGINE**
HALF-A-CAN HALF-A-MO HUMMUS

Introduction

I'm gazing out of the wide front window of our little wooden house onto Brevig Bay. The sea is choppy and the clouds scud southward. The east cardinal buoy tip-tilts on the edge of the shipping lane and the mainland-bound ferry heads resolutely for the horizon. It's August and just after eight in the morning, too cold and windy for any sightseer to remain on deck, so nobody notices the sea eagle flapping nonchalantly past.

Every time we wake to this view we pinch ourselves: our dreams came true when we married and moved here. It's a completely different life, far away from the stresses of crowds, commuting and working. With around a thousand residents, we're a safe community where everyone's known and we wave to each other as we drive past on the circular single-track road that encircles the isle in just twelve miles.

We spend a lot of time outside, whatever the weather's doing – and it does a lot here – high winds, heavy rains, spells of beautiful sunshine, often all in the same week! We come home to a wood-burning stove and the entertainments of the internet, shelves of books and our simple kitchen. Our menu isn't influenced by TV bake-offs and our timetable doesn't revolve around talent shows, because we've got no TV. We like it that way. We relish our remoteness and delight in being different.

But wherever you live, you want nice food. Preferably a good variety of it too. The choice is limited here on the beautiful isle of Barra. Supplies can be unreliable: most of us keep a stash of groceries for the days the boat doesn't make it, the power goes off, unexpected guests turn up or the freezer breaks down. We're resourceful cooks who network ideas and share our skills. I still revel in the randomness of what's left in the shop by the end of the day and what I can make with it, so this book is a celebration of needs-must creativity. Things don't always turn out as expected, as you'll read, but I learned from the fails and moved on, a more experienced dinner dabbler.

I'm not a chef. I'm not even a very good cook. I want to eat wholesome stuff and know what's in it, but not spend too much time or money on food. I've got a life outside of the kitchen after all, and ours would be regarded by many as woefully basic. My propane gas cooker has just one shelf and poor controllability. The microwave is second-hand and cheap. Energy prices are high: we use only cold water in the kitchen and bathroom sinks, washing our hands and washing up our dishes (perfectly well) under the cold tap. We're in the top ten most expensive places in the UK, and indeed in Europe, to get petrol, which of course pushes up the price of anything that's delivered. We've no dishwasher, an elderly washing machine and no tumble dryer. But compared to so many in the world, we're rich. We live in a safe place among a supportive community. I know from the many hitch-hiking trips I've made around the planet that there are far worse places to be. I learned so much on my adventures: about people, about looking after myself, and about being accepted at face value and giving the same back. While travelling, I ate a lot of things I'd never tried before, and some of those international recipes are in this book. The people who were kind and hospitable towards me were, for the most part, not wealthy at all, which was a definite plus as I got to see what life was really like in other countries, without the blinkers a package tour provides or seclusion in the blandly generic kind of hotel many of the locals couldn't afford to enter. Poorer people have to get on with making a living as well as eating, so they can't spend all day faffing around the kitchen. I took some time, fuel and money-saving tips away with me and I've used them ever since.

I like being creative with food though I don't want to spend my life doing it: an hour of hovering over the stove has me losing the will to live. We all want to eat every day, so the person tasked with cooking has to think of something, preferably new, different and exciting, *every single day*. And it's not just the planning and serving: it's the shopping, the preparing, the cleaning up afterwards and the time and head-space all of that takes. Somewhere during that process, probably when someone notices they're hungry, you'll be asked what's for dinner. *You don't have to say!* It's like when you've chosen your unborn child's name or your next book's theme but you keep it to yourself because you don't want the input of others. Tell them it's a surprise. This is a handy tactic if the person asking is prone to eye-rolling or nose-upturning when they hear what's coming. Unless they take over the *whole* process, *every single day,* of planning, shopping, paying, cooking, serving and cleaning up, they don't get the opportunity to spoil a meal before it's even on the stove. The family may be away on holiday, or enjoying a lazy Sunday, or doing something else they like, but they'll still be expecting to eat. And on high days and holidays they expect to eat something superior to the usual. I know a lot of people who say they love cooking, but on the rare occasions they do it they make one of their special signature dishes which everyone praises to the skies. They expect, like a TV chef, to walk into a kitchen fully stocked and ready for them, eventually walking out of it again leaving chaos behind for someone else to deal with. They use every utensil in the kitchen and leave them all dirty. They interrupt the regular cook at intervals by asking, "Is there any...?" A real cook works *every day* and knows what's in the kitchen and what isn't because they've planned, bought, stocked up, prepared and stock-rotated by date. Not only that, but they take responsibility for the health and wellbeing of everyone they cook for. Every day. Pete Wells, who wrote a column for the New York Times called 'Cooking with Dexter' as a busy working father preparing food for his son, admitted in his final piece that he'd actually done very little cooking. His wife did the daily drudgery because he didn't have the time. They were both full-time workers, but she sacrificed hours when she could have been making money for the sake of the family. Does that ring bells with anyone?

I'd better add right now that my husband Bruce is more than happy to pull his weight in the kitchen. Furthermore, he expertly grows many of the ingredients in our small garden and cheerfully goes out in the dark or the rain to dig up or pick and wash whatever's needed for dinner. The sandy soil is fertilised with seaweed we collect from the beach and haul up to dig into the growing beds over the winter. Super-fresh vegetables, rinsed under the hose outside, trimmed up before they're brought in: we're lucky to have those while the brief growing season permits, and we preserve as much as we can. Bruce makes a mean leek and potato soup, with everything from the garden thrown in, and that's the kind of thing we can keep in the freezer for leaner times. It's a small fridge-freezer though, and sooner or later it'll die on us. After feasting our way through everything left in it, we'd head back to the storecupboard.

So this is a book of easy recipes, quick to make from inexpensive everyday ingredients that transform a can from the cupboard into something surprisingly different: putting the fun back into the functional!

Everyone wishes there were ready meals available that could replace home cooking without being fingered as causing obesity or nutritional deficiency. 'Processing' has become a dirty word. But as any cook knows, processing is what we do. Scratch cooking is processing. Baking is processing. Processing is hard work and if we don't do it, you take your chances with what a factory has done for you. Time is what we want: time we don't have because we have to work, or time we want to enjoy somewhere other than by the sink. Ready-prepared, portioned-out, peeled, cooked, hygienic, tidy, calorie-counted, nutrition-listed cans take some of that drudgery away. That's the kind of factory processing I'm happy with, to save my precious time and make my food prepping more efficient. From a can, I only need to do the pleasurable bit: thinking of something to create from my quality-assured ingredients, quickly and simply. I bear the cost in mind and look out for reduced items to throw in before they're past their use-by date, saving them from wastage and make sure the cooking isn't too much of a palaver. Once it's in the oven you can be doing something else, setting a timer for when it needs looking at next. If it's a dessert or something to refrigerate or leave to stand, once it's done, you don't need to think about it until you're hungry.

Joan Collins once said, "We should celebrate being women and having the opportunities to do things that our mothers and grandmothers were not allowed to do. They were expected to stay at home and do the cooking and the cleaning. Though now, of course, we are expected to do the cooking and the cleaning and the working." I like her attitude. That's why I don't waste *my* time on too much of what I don't want to do.

I have friends who take Sandals-type holidays when they go away: you wear a wristband to a buffet and choose whatever you fancy. Nobody has to make a decision. Similarly, my randomly picked can per day is a way of opting out of the relentless menu-making process, just doing my best with what I've got, almost as though there was a war on!

We've few eating-out options to give the cook a day off: three hotels do expensive versions of things-and-chips, or there's a lovely curry restaurant with limited opening days and times. Apart from that we have a bowl of soup in a café, visit neighbours or wait for the opportunity of a trip off the island to provide a change. This challenge, then, is simply to maintain my interest in cooking and to entertain myself until we get away to sample a different lifestyle and cuisine. A change is as good as a rest, they say. Invariably, before much time has elapsed, we're more than ready to return to our island idyll.

When we moved here, shrugging off the responsibilities and challenges of our jobs before we got too old to appreciate our freedom, I gained the time to play and the opportunity to daydream. So why not play with my food?

I decided to take on this project as an experiment in resourcefulness in uncertain times. A hundred days, going from high summer into autumnal gales and the relentless approach of winter, is a decent chunk of time which highlights how many of the aspects of our new life are different from those we left behind. It gave me enough time to get through just about every kind of vegetarian tinned food on the island and a few more unusual cans from the mainland as well!

Those cans made a hundred and twenty recipes, noted day by day as the weeks went on. There were a few of our tried-and-tested old favourites among them, but many were new to us: playful inventions from my imagination, adapted from recipes I'd read or been told about, or dishes I'd enjoyed while travelling the world, customised to accommodate the availability – or lack – of ingredients here.

Talking of availability, I'll now confess to what is and isn't in my pantry. Some things I don't buy because I wouldn't use them enough and they'd spoil, some can't be obtained here, and others I'm just too bone idle to bother with. So before you look at my recipes, I'd better let you know what you're in for…

It's granulated sugar unless otherwise stated: I don't buy caster sugar or brown sugars as they're expensive and soon turn into a block in the damp. If a recipe needs darker sugar I can always add a bit of black treacle or golden syrup.

I always buy self-raising flour and use it for everything, even bread: it's 95p for 1.5kg in our shop and if I just keep one type of flour in, it's never there long enough to go stale. I never sift it either: I don't think it matters a jot to the finished result!

I never make puff pastry (I buy it when it's reduced to clear in the supermarket chilled section, then freeze it) but always make easy-peasy shortcrust.

If a cake or loaf calls for a beaten egg, I just break an egg into the mixture and stir it in. "Aha! What if it's a bad egg?" I hear my 1970s Domestic Science teacher cry. Well, I've bought two bad eggs in my whole long life. If I count up the time I've *not* spent beating eggs in separate bowls which I would've then had to wash up along with the beating implements, I reckon I've come out ahead here. I use grammes and millilitres for measurements, and sometimes a pinch, dash or splash if it's not too critical, or up to the individual's taste or dietary preferences, how much of something goes in.

I try to use centimetres for recipes but old habits die hard, so feet and inches are still in my vocabulary too.

I use margarine rather than butter as it's a lot cheaper and also vegan-friendly if you pick the right brand. I get a 2kg tub (from the mainland, brought over by prevailed-upon guests) suitable for baking and spreading and use it for everything except frying. If I ran out of oil I would fry in suitable margarine, taking care not to let it get too hot.

My cooking oil is just the cheapest brand, with olive oil saved for dressings etc.

I cook with the very cheapest cheese from Aldi or Lidl. They charge the same for grated or block cheese, so I rarely grate my own. If there was a block of cheese in the fridge that had gone hard, I'd likely grate it then freeze it or use it up in cooking straightaway. Likewise, if I found block cheese at a bargain price, I'd use what I could and freeze the rest for another time.

I don't always use the given temperature in a recipe if other things are being baked at the same time; I move the food higher or lower within the oven, checking how it's doing, and if possible turning it off sooner than the recipe advises, leaving the door closed for a while to continue the cooking process with the residual heat. I save precious fuel and money that way. The one thing I really, really like about my oven, which I've never had before, is the glass door and interior light. I can watch over things without opening the door and letting the heat out, although I confess I'm not obsessive about keeping that glass panel clean. ("Shame on you!" mutters my cookery teacher over my shoulder.) Bear in mind that I cook with propane gas: it heats quickly but burns with more moisture than an electric oven. This means it needs to be a bit hotter for crunchy and crispy foods and the dish needs to be high up to get the top brown. I don't pre-heat the oven if I don't need to, e.g. for roasted vegetables, casseroles and anything else that doesn't have to rise courtesy of flour or eggs. Since it's a small appliance, I often start with something that doesn't need a pre-heated oven and whip that out once done to replace it with something that does, such as a cake or loaf.

So with all my cooking temperatures and times, go with your own experience and watch and smell how things are doing. You can be getting on with something else, just keeping one eye on what's baking!

In these recipes I list the ingredients followed by the method unless it's a really simple process (and a lot of them are dead easy) in which case I just highlight the ingredients you need as I go through the step-by-step instructions. So here we go: a hundred days of cans in the kitchen!

A hundred days: the diary

Day 1: Friday 3rd August

First day of the challenge, and I've installed a box in the hallway behind an old easy chair. It's full of cans, listed and alphabetised so that each corresponds to a Scrabble tile from A to Z in a bag put aside for the purpose. I fish within it, produce a letter, and find what I'll be cooking with each day.

I'd been wondering how cans came to be invented. We now take them entirely for granted wherever we shop, but there must have been a demand for them in the first place. Reading up on the origin of one of our commonest food sources, I discovered their engaging history.

In the late eighteenth century's population boom, as people shifted to urban centres in the industrial revolution, they needed safe supplies of food. Pickling, salting or drying was too expensive to do on a large scale, and these new town-dwellers no longer had the time or land to produce their own food. The world was ready for a new invention.

In 1795 the French government offered a cash reward (worth about £500 at the time) to anyone who could provide preserved food for Napoleon's army. A confectioner, Nicolas Appert, developed a process of heating glass jars of meat, fruit and vegetables in water at up to 100 degrees Celsius, which sterilised the contents and kept them (usually) safe with an airtight seal. His preserved fruits saved the French navy from scurvy, and he won his prize money in 1810. Louis Pasteur later improved on his methods by heating to a temperature of 70 degrees, which kept more flavour while killing enough bacteria to render the food safe. The sealing of the jars was improved in 1859 by J.L. Mason, who used a tough metal lid and screw-top.

Another Frenchman, Denis Papin, had invented the pressure cooker in the 17th century, and his work on speedy, safe cooking was further improved in the 1800s by Charles Chamberland's development of Appert's autoclave. Sterilising food under pressure means that preservatives are unnecessary so the flavour is unaffected.

A condition of Appert's reward was that he published his research, and *L'Art de conserver...* is still available on Amazon today. His seventh edition explains how fish was preserved in tins in Nantes, and the tins opened with a soldering iron. In spite of his pioneering work and many awards in his lifetime, Appert died a pauper. Pierre Durand, a Frenchman living in Britain, got hold of his book and was spurred to sell his own patent for preserved food in metal cans to a trio of British businessmen, Donkin, Hall and Gamble, for a thousand pounds. The original wrought-iron cans were heavy and hard to open: a hammer and chisel was recommended to get into one brand, while soldiers attacked them with their bayonets. Opening cans remained a problem until 1925, when the modern opener with a key and a pair of cutting wheels at last became available. Tin made cans lighter and more durable, and the British navy benefited from the new supplies. One 19th century Admiral ordered 'soup and bouilli' for his men: preserved meat with gravy, from which the term 'bully beef' is thought to have originated. From hand-made tins sealed with toxic lead solder we gradually moved on to mechanised production and thinner metal, easier to cut into. In the early days the best craftsmen could only make 6 cans an hour, whereas now machines turn out 6-800 per minute. Problems of rusting were solved by galvanising the cans, and eventually plastic-lined tins solved the problem of a tinny taste when the contents, such as tomatoes, were acidic. All these improvements led to the popularity of convenient canned foods today. Anywhere you go in the world, however remote or poverty-stricken, you can rely on safe, affordable food that keeps for years, thanks to the humble can that once kept soldiers fighting fit.

First recipe off the blocks: and behold, it's that old staple, Heinz beans. In a way I'm relieved it's something familiar to cut my teeth on, but in another it's so predictable, something we have every week anyway, that I can't for the life of me think of a different way to use them. They go in our curries and soups or turn up on toast or baked potatoes, but mostly they accompany our hot Sunday breakfast. What on earth can I do with them that's just a wee bit different?

After a busy morning's gardening, Bruce and I went off to the airport to watch the wading birds. It was a lovely day, dry enough to get our washing done for the first time in a week. My attention didn't turn to dinner until we were at last heading for home.

Scots make bridies with a meaty filling from shortcrust or puff pastry, and Cubans sell puff pastry *pastelitos*, sweet or savoury pasties often containing cheese, on many a street corner. The deli shelf of our supermarket sports a bean and cheese slice for around £2 as a convenience food, but I reckoned I could do something like that cheaper and better at home. So I did.

BEAN AND CHEESE BRIDIES

A can of baked beans, with some of the liquid drained off
A good handful of grated cheese
Ready-made puff pastry from the fridge
A bit of flour for rolling out

Pre-heat the oven: gas 6, 200C/400F
Dust a bit of flour on your work surface. Roll the pastry into a large oblong (you can use a bottle if you haven't got a rolling pin), cut in half and spoon a heap of beans just to the left of the centre on each piece of pastry. Top with cheese.
Fold the pastry over onto the filling and squash down the edges of each "parcel" firmly with a fork. Make a few fork holes in the centre of each parcel.
Slide the parcels carefully onto a greased baking tray and put on an upper oven shelf.
Have a look at the slices after 20 minutes. Remove when they're golden on top.
Enjoy with chips or mash, or leave to cool and take out as a packed lunch.

Day 2: Saturday 4th August

I spent my day helping out as a kitchen assistant, preparing all kinds of food for the next night: a 5-course banquet was being held for a whole coach-load of VIP diners, so there was plenty to do. That day I made sandwiches for fifty people's lunch. We were short of mayo, which creates a more spreadable sandwich filling out of chicken, roast veg. or tuna, but I improvised by spinning it out with oil. There were two cauldrons of soup too, and we were gratified to see everything eagerly scarfed away. Once we'd washed up and done as much as possible towards the big event to come, I went home to be greeted by my modest can of the day: European brown lentils. It was nice to have them all ready to go without weighing, soaking or boiling of pulses to fuss with. I knocked up a loaf in ten minutes flat, including picking and washing the chives. I didn't pre-heat the oven: I just turned it on, bunged the tin inside and went for a shower. When I emerged, I cooked up some carrots and used the water they were boiled in to make Bisto gravy, which, pleasingly, is vegan.

My recipe was loosely based on one in the book Bruce got for his 21st birthday: Linda McCartney's Home Cooking. It's still a handy collection of ideas although it relied heavily on 1980s textured vegetable protein, cream and crumbled-up veggieburgers. Different times of course, but it provided the inspiration I needed for our retro main course.

LENTIL HERBY LOAF

1 can of drained brown lentils

115g grated cheddar
chopped chives, a handful
a pinch each of salt and black pepper
1 tsp mixed dried herbs
55g breadcrumbs
1 beaten egg
45g margarine, warmed up a little

Mix the lentils with the cheese, chives and seasoning.
Add the breadcrumbs, egg and margarine. Mix together and add more breadcrumbs if the mix is sloppy. It should be like thick porridge.
Pour into a greased tin or dish.
Bake at gas 4, 180C/350F, for 30 mins or until it's cooked through and brown on top.

Day 3: Sunday 5th August

It was a busy day to continue my challenge. Up early on a Sunday morning as usual, I scraped back my hair and sorted out an apron. I don't own one, so I chose my cleanest tea-towel and hastily sewed tapes onto the top and sides to tie it on with. A tin of cooked new potatoes turned out to be our can today, which was great as I'd be short on time and patience later! I made Bruce a couple of sandwiches for lunch with a bit of potato salad on the side, and set off at half past nine.

A full day ensued preparing the feast for the clan MacNeil: members were visiting from every corner of the globe for their biennial gathering. They had a big menu: soup, paté, roast dinner and stuffing (all with vegetarian options) followed by desserts, then confectionery and a wee dram or two. There was traditional live music and plenty of speeches, toasts and banter: the crowd looked fine in their handsome blue-and-green tartan. In spite of the demands of the dishwasher and the pressing need to keep the platefuls going out hot to the tables, we workers had time to enjoy the event and have a laugh. It was an unforgettable experience and all the foreign visitors were appreciative. By the time we were done, we were all worn out, but it was definitely worthwhile.

Late that night I stuck a pizza in the oven and served it up with the rest of the spuds prepared as in the recipe below. I couldn't face cooking anything else, but I'd been given a couple of opened bottles of red wine that the diners hadn't finished, and somehow we found the energy to deal with those.

SWIFT POTATO SALAD

Drain **a tin of new potatoes** well, cut them into bite-sized pieces and toss in **2-3 tbsp vegan mayo,** (see day 7) salad cream or mayonnaise, a few **snipped chives** and **black pepper** to taste. If not using the salad straightaway, keep it in the fridge but take out half an hour before serving to bring up to room temperature.

Serve with pizza and plenty of wine.

Day 4: Monday 6th August

I did some emailing to invite our neighbours to a little get-together the next Friday night, to celebrate the beginning of my latest project. I was deliberately light on detail, asking them to come for cheese and wine, and not to bring anything except for a can of something vegetarian. They're tolerant of my unusual ways, but actually the whole of our street is littered with delightful eccentrics. Have you ever sent your Christmas cards in July to beat the rush? Do you keep your taramasalata in a teapot in the fridge? Do you buy carrots for the wild rabbits in the hope that they'll leave the plants in your garden alone? Neither do I. I rest my case.

The letter 'U' yielded a Co-op low-fat tomato and three bean soup as can of the day. I'm not a fan of low-fat anything: I think misguided 1970s advice on reducing fat intake to lose weight is one of the reasons the world is getting bigger. Fat doesn't make you fat: it makes you satisfied, and without it I, at least, feel colder, weaker and more likely to gorge on stodgy carbohydrates to fill the gap. Those carbs may not contain a lot of fat, but they've other properties that send your blood glucose soaring, only to crash a couple of hours later. I wanted the tin to do for two of us, too. There was only one thing to do, then, with the offending soup:

FULLY FATISFYING LUNCHTIME SOUP

One can of 'low fat' tomato and three bean soup
A big glug of olive oil

Half a dozen fresh or over-ripe tomatoes with the skin peeled off (drop the toms in boiling water, then it's easy)
Basil, fresh or dried
Black pepper
A squirt of tomato ketchup or some tomato purée

Put everything in the pan to heat up, mashing down the tomatoes with a potato masher. Stir well and taste, adjusting the seasoning if necessary. Serve with a well-spread slice of wholemeal toast.

Day 5: Tuesday 7th August

The mystery tin today revealed itself to be apricot halves. Hmm. We love juicy dried apricots, and we love Archers peach liqueur. In Somerset, Bruce's lucky sister has an amazingly prolific apricot tree from which she produces sorbet and delicious jam. But we never, ever buy the fruit tinned. It brings back childhood memories of a puddle of fruit and liquid straight from the tin with a begrudging splash of evaporated milk curdling in the middle of it. Or greyish, metallic-tasting sterilised cream. I'd probably have liked condensed milk as a kid, but we never had it. To add insult to injury, up at the top of our road, half a mile away on the edge of town, was a small old-fashioned dairy farm. They sold their produce straight from the yard, but we never got to taste it.

As an ironic nod to my 1970s teenage years, when yogurt was an exotic food viewed by my parents with deep suspicion, I served Bruce some with a solitary apricot half embedded in it at lunchtime. For the evening, I had a much more exciting dish to prepare, with only three ingredients! My kind of cooking. Based on Afro-Caribbean cornbread with a hint of Australian johnnycake, this surprisingly delicious cake is a fusion of a couple of recipes I encountered on my travels once I finally left grim Thatcherite England and began to explore.

APRICOT PONE CAKE

Pour **a tin of apricot halves** (411g) and its juice into a bowl. Blend smooth with a stick blender then stir in 185g

flour and 75g **sugar**. Pour into a shallow greased ovenproof tin or dish.

Bake on gas 4, 350F/180C for around 30 min, testing if cooked by checking if a knife blade comes out clean when inserted in the cake's centre.

Serve warm or cold. Can be dusted with icing sugar or spread with cupcake icing when cool.

Day 6: Wednesday 8th August

Bruce works part-time at the polytunnel project, an educational scheme on the island. He grows bedding plants and shrubs, year-round lettuce, the necessities for preserves, jams and chutneys, onions, beans, purple mange tout and many more surprising fruit and veg, given our inhospitable conditions. After a heavy morning's volunteering with him, spraying mare's tails (the weed, not the ponies) with white vinegar in the hope of killing them dead, picking and planting and generally lending a hand, I went home to today's can: Homepride curry. I usually buy cooking sauces in a jar, resenting the price when I know that Asda sells a jar of curry sauce for just 30p, and the cheapest jar over here is 75p. So paying almost twice that for a can of the same stuff didn't come easily: I just hoped it would be somehow superior. It seems quite dated to have it in a can these days: I think consumers prefer jars because they like to see the colour of the contents through the glass. In taste and colour, it wasn't dissimilar to Chinese or Japanese curry sauce, quite mild and heavy on the turmeric. I used to like a ladleful of such a sauce over my sandcastle-shaped mound of rice in cheap Japanese cafeterias.

I Googled recipes for more unusual curry dishes. Chocolate curry cupcakes, anyone? The recipe said they suit people 'with an open mind'. But you also need at least 45 minutes and about a dozen ingredients, including erythritol, which I'd never even heard of before. It's a sweetener which even in small doses can cause side effects including diarrhoea. So for those curry cupcakes, as well as the open mind, you'd better have a few spare rolls of toilet paper!

I decided to stick with my own recipe. It was an easy dish to create and took all of five minutes to do. I had some frozen rice left over from a takeaway in the freezer, so I took it out and stir-fried it, still frozen, in a well-oiled pan as the curry was heating. An easy dinner that hits the spot.

QUICK CAN CURRY

Pour **a can of curry** into a pan, rinsing it so as not to waste any residue. While heating, throw in a handful of **frozen mixed veg**. Add any **leftover vegetables** you like: I put in diced cooked potatoes with the skin on, some baked beans including their sauce, and a few previously roasted courgette and carrot chunks from the fridge. Put the lid on the pan and let it heat up. While it was heating, I picked a few **spinach** and **chard** leaves from the garden, rinsed and chopped them and threw them on top of the curry. Stir well before serving over rice.

Day 7: Thursday 9th August

Can of the Day, letter W from the Scrabble bag, was chickpeas. I had a vague memory of a recipe our vegan friends Josh and Charlie had shown us two Augusts ago, when they came up in their camper-van to get married on Vatersay Beach. It rained every day of their ten-day stay, but miraculously the sun came out for the ceremony, after which we all jumped into a *really* cold sea.

For dinner, I added some of the chickpeas to yesterday's leftover curry and served it on a bed of ready-made ginger noodles. Quick and easy (chick-)peasy. That was useful as I had some cleaning up to do for our party the following day, including finally sorting out the laundry and bedding from our last visitor, who went home almost a month before...

So lunchtime was the chance for that little can to show its mettle (pun intended). I was utilising 'aquafaba', the liquid surrounding chickpeas in a can, which is high in protein and too useful just to throw away. I'd been told, though I'd never tried it, that you can use it in sponge cakes or pancakes to make them lighter without adding eggs, or even whip it up like a meringue. Something to do when I had a bit more time and energy! Charlie did the most amazing vegan ginger cake for their wedding breakfast, as well as loads of other fabulous dishes while they stayed with us. More traditionally, this lunchtime I did boiled-egg sandwiches and enlivened them with the following:

CHARLIE'S VEGAN MAYO

4 tablespoons water from a can of chickpeas

20 chickpeas
1 tablespoon lemon juice
a pinch of salt
250ml oil

Put everything except the oil into the narrow plastic jug you get with a stick blender.

Pour the oil on top of the other ingredients.

Put the blender into the bottom of the jug, turn it on, and as the liquid thickens and whitens, gradually lift the blender upwards. It only takes a few seconds: don't over-blend.

You can add Dijon mustard, chilli flakes or other seasonings if you fancy it.

Dead easy and delicious; it keeps for a few days in the fridge.

Day 8: Friday 10th August

I was volunteering at Bruce's workplace all morning, picking beautifully fresh salads and vegetables and preparing them for sale that afternoon in the community shop in Castlebay. We proudly laid out the washed lettuce leaves, kale and special varieties of tomato, having seen them safely all the way from seed to shop. They were naturally grown and sure to be delicious. How absurd it seemed, at the height of the growing season with abundance all around us, to be eating from tins. But not every day offers such a bounty.

Once showered and recovered, I laid out the cheese and wine for my cans and canapés evening and opened today's can: mixed bean salad. In honour of our guests, I was making nibbles with it, alongside the Applewood and Edam (gifts from our previous house guest) and Mousetrap (our purchase from Aldi). I washed up as I went along: since we don't use hot tap water, I've perfected the art. My tactic is to use a sponge scourer containing a few drops of neat washing-up liquid, and not to leave things hanging around until the food dries. When collecting plates after a meal, I don't stack them: that makes extra work by putting food onto both sides of the dishes instead of just the one. I dry up afterwards, which allows a second look at each piece for quality-control purposes. Donald Schaffner, a food scientist from Rutgers University in the U.S., recently published the results of a study in the *Journal of Food Protection* showing that hand-washing in cold water is as effective as in hot. Although washing up isn't mentioned, he does point out that using cold water could have significant energy-saving implications. A fifth of Russian city dwellings have no hot water at all, and it's estimated that over 40% of the world at large doesn't. This makes me appreciate our electric shower much more!

Tonight was a low-maintenance evening. I'd got away with not creating dessert thanks to a couple of lemon meringue pies reduced to 88p each, and with not buying any wine as we'd been given bottles by all of our visitors over the summer. So, including my 'new' dress from the thrift shop, the whole evening cost us around a tenner.

The guests started to arrive at seven. They were curious to hear about my project, and I was pleased they'd turned out to support me. Wine in hand, they listened politely as I explained my exercise in resourcefulness and indicated the line of tins on the windowsill with tea-lights flickering on the top. Everyone had brought a tin of something vegetarian as requested, and I got them to swap it for one of mine. During this process I somehow became the owner of a tin of haggis, that lesser-known veggie dish. Hmmm, a conundrum for another day! Another couple of wags had taken the labels off their cans, just to make my life more interesting, but apart from that we got beansprouts, green beans, cider, kidney beans, peas, and a poem about peas. Yes, I know, but she did bring a tin as well. Soup was a popular choice that the guests put aside to take home: handy for lunch I suppose and not requiring any further treatment to turn it into a meal. The cherry pie filling went too, and one brave soul, Lee, pocketed one of the several un-labelled cans. He liked it because of the Chinese characters stamped on the top, and we made him promise to let us know what it was and what he did with it.

"So what are you doing with all the cans? Are you going to recycle them all?" asked Tara as I topped everyone up again.

"I've been looking at ideas on YouTube. I can make a Valentine rose from a drinks can..."

"You'll make it red as soon as you cut yourself," said Bruce helpfully.

"It's true, you need to be super-tough for some of the ideas. But then there's a way to make stilts from two cans..." I continued enthusiastically.

"This is going to be the most *boring* book," groaned Gina over her wine glass.

"-And I've got stories - Canecdotes - about the history of canning..."

"Are you explaining why some cans have ring-pulls and some don't?" asked Travis.

"Yes, and different ways to open a can without an opener!" I gushed.

"This is going to be the *most boring book...*" said Gina, rolling her eyes.

Ignoring her scepticism, I explained how one fingers-of-steel YouTube contributor opens cans with a spoon, a fork, a knife or his bare hands, and how a guy calling himself 'Mission Survivor' scrubbed his can on a concrete step until the seal on top gave way, allowing him to access the gritty, metal-shard-contaminated contents. But if you're a survivalist, the grit's probably a bonus. The only problem we could foresee with that is where you find your concrete step in the middle of the woods, or in the Gobi desert. Perhaps he carries one. Instead of a tin opener.

So the evening went on, with much hilarity and speculation. My peculiar nibbles were cautiously nibbled, recipes were suggested and shared, and cans were carried and tins toted homeward to be turned into who knows what. I was officially out of the closet with my culinary craziness and would be asked how it was going at intervals over the next few weeks. It was a bit like going on a diet: you tell everyone so they'll remind you of it and keep you on track, even when you don't feel as motivated as you did on Day One. Their interest would encourage me on days when there were other preoccupations, and perhaps at the end of it I'd even be a better, or at least a more efficient, cook.

SPICY BEAN CUPS

6 slices medium or thin sliced bread, preferably 3 white, 3 brown
a bit of margarine
a can of mixed bean salad, drained
a dollop of mayonnaise (or vegan mayo, see Day 7)
chilli sauce, e.g. Tabasco

Grease a 12-hole bun tin and pre-heat the oven on 4, 350F/180C. Cut 2 discs from each slice of bread with a cookie cutter, freezing the other bits of the slices in a bag to make breadcrumbs another day. Spread the discs with a little margarine and press firmly into the bun tin. Put 3 or 4 beans from the can into each cup and press down.

Bake until toasted golden: they should only take a few minutes to do. Meanwhile, mix the rest of the beans with mayo and a dash of chilli sauce to taste. Once the cups are done, leave to cool in the bun tin then fill with the beans in dressing. Just before serving, arrange on a plate with other nibbles. Serve with wine.

Day 9: Saturday 11th August

After a hard afternoon's birding on Vatersay, looking at an American ring-billed gull on a deserted beach, we returned home tired and hungry. Lee had suggested we made an omelette when I ceremonially drew the letter for his tin of green beans at yesterday's party. He bemoaned the lack of asparagus tips on the island, which is what he'd wanted to bring along. He'd even tried asking at the local hotel, just in case they had a secret supply or even a giant catering can of some kind of vegetable, but he came away empty-handed. In recognition of his efforts beyond the call of duty, I decided to make the omelette a bit less prosaic, more like the tapas I used to have a soft spot for in bars in Barcelona.

SPANISH CAN-ISH TORTILLA

A couple of cooked potatoes
A clove of crushed garlic
Chopped chives (because I didn't have any onions)
Some leftover kidney beans and chickpeas
Dried mixed herbs
A handful of grated cheese
A can of green beans, well drained
4 eggs, beaten
A splash of oil

In a small non-stick pan with rounded edges, preferably not too deep, fry the cooked potatoes and arrange evenly around the bottom of the pan. Sprinkle the garlic among them then combine the other ingredients and pour over the spuds. Put a lid on the pan and cook over a medium heat, keeping an eye on it. When it starts to firm up, smooth the liquid egg towards the edges of the pan with a spatula until the surface of the tortilla is cooked. Turn off the heat, replace the lid and leave to stand for a minute, then get a plate and hold it firmly face down over the top of the pan. Turn everything upside down and hopefully the tortilla will plop out in one piece onto the plate. You can cut slices into it like a cake, and serve it hot or cold with rice, couscous or chips. Any veg work well in this: red peppers arranged between the potatoes in the pan bottom look fabulous when you tip the tortilla out.

Day 10: Sunday 12th August

After a cloudy start, it rained buckets all afternoon. Once the supermarket opened at 12.30, I struggled through the puddly car park with my heavy shopping, since Sunday is an opportunity to carry things home in our car. On weekdays when Bruce is working, I take my backpack and buy anything else we need, or any bargains the reduced-price shelf offers up. Suitably set up for the week, I made some mashed potato while tonight's creation baked. I do mash by microwaving whole spuds, peeling them while still hot, then smashing with a fork with added margarine. They stay hot for ages.

My sister-in-law Sarah makes a divine version of this dish for visiting vegetarians, with home-cooked and mostly home-grown ratatouille ingredients. Here's mine, without the TLC but considerably faster in consequence. Did you know that the name comes from the French verb *'touiller'*, meaning 'to stir up'? Or that it's called Valentine in southern France or Piperade in the Basque region? I'm sure Sarah does. But it was news to me when I picked out our can for today.

RATATOUILLE PIE

170g flour

85g margarine (I don't measure these two ingredients actually, just dump some flour in a bowl and add what feels like half the flour's weight in marge. I rub in the fat, add just enough water to bind it, and hey presto, a lump of shortcrust pastry)

A small pack of puff pastry, or more shortcrust made as above if you haven't any

A tin of ratatouille

Pre-heat the oven on gas 6, 400F/200C. Grease a pie or flan dish of about 10". Roll out the shortcrust and line the dish, and roll out and measure a lid for the pie out of the puff pastry or shortcrust, whichever you're using. Put the pastry lid on a plate and put it in the fridge while you bake the lined dish blind for 10 mins or so. I don't prick it with a fork first or put in baking beans, and it comes out fine.

Bring out the partly cooked pie base, pour the can of cold ratatouille onto it, and position the pastry lid. Crimp it down with a fork and make a few fork holes in the top, then return to the oven. Take a look at it after 20 mins and bring it out when the top is golden brown. If you didn't have enough pastry for a lid, you could do a bit of a lattice on the top, or just do it as a tart with a sprinkling of cheese or breadcrumbs: those options would be ready a bit sooner. Serve with mash. We had rainbow chard in the garden so I steamed a bit of that and served everything with instant vegetarian gravy made from the water I'd used for the steaming.

Day 11: Monday 13th August

It's the third day in a row that the freezers have been empty in the supermarket. I'd asked if there were any frozen vegetables in the back of the store the Friday before, and was told that the freezers had all broken down and the contents had been thrown away. Thrown in the bin! I understand that retailers have to keep to strict rules about storing food, and that if the freezer or fridge temperatures stray beyond their limits in either direction then that food can't be sold, for health and safety reasons. But let's bear in mind that a customer might live some distance away from the store, so the manufacturers have to allow for a journey home in the packaging of frozen food. According to the FoodSafety website, as long as the frozen food still contains ice crystals, it's safe to re-freeze. And in our climate it's not going to defrost quickly. I wish they'd given it away over the course of the hour after the freezers broke down by mentioning it to people at the till or putting up a sign or a Facebook message. Some of it, such as pizzas, fish, bakery items and sausages, would have been fine to cook from thawed anyway, even if the pack says the best results are obtained when cooked from frozen. It upsets me to think of all that stuff, which needed all that precious energy to process it and ship it here, being dumped *in the bin.* I could only guess that the powers that be might have objected, or there were fears that they would, or the hard-working staff just didn't have time to find out. Anyway, my staples of frozen peas and emergency oven chips have already run out, so it's lucky I've got a lot of tins in! On top of that, the power supply has been particularly unreliable recently. It's to be expected in winter, when poles get blown down and the grid experiences a high demand. Two Christmas Eves ago, Bruce found a power line sparking and shorting out: it had been struck by lightning and the cables were hanging from a broken pole. He took a photo and showed the local Scottish Hydro guy, who heroically went out into the storm in the dark to save a lot of people's big roast dinner.

In high summer, however, nobody expects the power to fail. Nor did we expect every household to receive a letter from our energy supplier apologising for the series of cuts we'd had in July: the consensus was that they recognised that we might switch suppliers, so felt duty-bound to explain themselves. Unfortunately, since the letter, some customers were notified again about times when the power would be off for maintenance work, but others weren't. Some were then told the times had changed, and Bruce seemed to be the only one who got a text saying the electricity would go down sometime between 9 and 5 that day. I passed the word around in the morning, prepared dinner, and left it sitting in the slow cooker.

Gina, at my can party, suggested this one-pot dinner for her can of butter beans. It was a dish she'd used for years as a welcome for people coming off the ferry: she said it didn't matter if the boat was late as the casserole was very forgiving. The recipe had slipped her mind that night, but I found something like it on the website of A Girl Called Jack (a terrific source of budget meal ideas) and adapted it to fit my pantry.

BUTTER BEAN AND CIDER CASSEROLE

Half a can of cider (flat or leftover drink is fine)
A can of butter beans including their liquid
A can of drained processed peas
Powdered veg. stock or stock cube
Thyme or any other herbs you've got
A roughly chopped carrot
A few broad beans (from our garden, but any leftover veg can be added instead)
An onion, chopped and fried, with some crushed garlic added for the last couple of minutes of frying time

Fling everything into the slow cooker, stir in enough water to cover everything well, put the lid on and leave it on 'low' for a whole day if you like, but at least a couple of hours. Can also be simmered on the stove for an hour or longer. Test the carrot is cooked before serving; if so, you're hot to trot. Serve with crusty bread or mash and greens.

Day 12: Tuesday 14th August

The rain sluiced down as I set off over the hill to Castlebay. The sparrows were feeding their latest brood of young and looking very bedraggled as they did so. Now and then they'd shake themselves, sending a cloud of water droplets into the heavy air. Heaval, our highest peak, was invisible in the Scotch mist, and the eight o'clock ferry to the mainland had vanished as soon as it cleared the harbour. It was strangely quiet, the modest Barra rush hour muffled by the cloud as I splashed uphill, thinking of my warm corner of the Learning Centre and the cup of coffee I'd have when I arrived to start writing. I wrote on their computers to take advantage of faster internet speeds and a detached working environment: too many distractions at home! Tara pulled up and offered me a lift before I'd had time to get properly wet, saving me time as well as a soaking. Our neighbours are great: Bruce drives to work in the opposite direction, but on nine walks out of ten someone stops as I hike uphill to see if I'd like to jump into their car.

The time I saved not walking was productively used in the supermarket. I looked for bargains, and today the fresh pizzas were marked down. Bruce could have a non-experimental dinner for a change, as lunch consisted of the tin earmarked for today: mushy peas. We both love them, and on one shopping trip when we still lived in Somerset, I found a 'clearance' stack of them priced at just 4p a tin! There were 48 cans, and every one went into my trolley, for a total cost of less than £2. They soon got used up on one of my favourite five-minute soups, which we never tire of.

This is Erinn's pea poem from the can party:

On a tin of mushy peas
The sweet pea's scent is heaven-sent,
Le petit-pois is dainty,
And perfect in translucent pod
A garden pea is tasty.
Sugar-snap is all the rage
When mange-tout rules the day
Snow peas sow the sweetest peace
When armies hold their sway.
Your dried and hard old wrinkled pea
Wallows murky in the soup;
And then there's me, the marrowfat
And processed pea, the coup
de grâce in egg and chips
with bangers and with creamy mash,
with every kind of breaded fish
and best of all in meaty hash.
You connoisseurs of gourmandise,
My flavour makes me say
It's that thick, green and mushy sauce
That surely wins the day.

Thomas Jefferson, who found time to write the American Declaration of Independence as well as being a horticultural pioneer, grew dozens of kinds of peas and founded the Charlottesville pea contest: the first producer of the season to harvest some peas hosted a community dinner, with at least one dish containing his or her peas. I'd love to do that here! His "garden book" has 66 pages, 44 of which mention peas, and he records in it the record speed of his 1771 pea harvest, planted on 6 March and served on 30 May. Unusually for his time, he was mostly vegetarian. He was a great experimenter (nothing wrong with playing with your food) and is even credited with the invention of French fries! We use peas a lot. I wish we could grow them as quickly as Jefferson's up here: high winds and limited sunshine mean that things grow at a far slower rate on the Hebrides. But we love our home-grown veg, even though, or perhaps because, we can't rely on it all year round.

THREE P'S PRONTO SOUP

Peas: canned mushy peas.
Potato: instant mash, just a bit, or some leftover spuds, mashed.
Pepper: freshly ground, black.

Empty the **mushy peas** into a pan, refill the can with **hot water** and pour that into the pan along with any last scrapings of peas. Add plenty of **black pepper** as you bring the pan just up to the boil. Take it off the heat and stir in some **mash** until the soup has thickened to a consistency you like. Enjoy this satisfying Thick Green Pea Soup with crusty bread.

Day 13: Wednesday 15th August

After blending up our leftover butter bean casserole into a hearty soup, I turned my thoughts to the next can while stapling booklets together. A self-published Barra guide I wrote had run out again, so I was preparing a few more copies. The staples didn't always go through the paper properly and had to be pulled out and done again. I had cut fingers and a short temper by the time they were finished.

I'd been looking up online recipes in readiness for the cans I'd be repeating. Some sounded a bit weird and wacky, but I didn't want to do the obvious, and I was already using something I'd had already: as on day one, I had Heinz beans to play with today. And play would be the operative word, since the recipe I based my day's efforts on was designed for mums and their toddlers to create as a 'messy' kitchen activity.

When I travelled in China and other parts of Asia, sweet bean cakes, mostly made from adzuki beans, were commonplace, either home-made or bought as a snack in the corner shop. Perhaps I could make a savoury equivalent here in the Western Isles. I needed something quick, easy and off-the-wall after a hard session of stapling. What would Heston Blumenthal do?

<u>BAKED BEAN MUFFINS</u>

160g flour
half a teaspoon of baking powder
1 beaten egg
50 ml oil
220g can of beans
60g grated red cheese
a bit of water if needed

Grease a muffin tray, and pre-heat the oven at gas 4, 180C/350F.

Stir the oil, egg, beans and cheese into the dry ingredients, plus a dash of water if the mix seems too dry. Don't over-mix. Dollop into the muffin tray and bake for around 20 min until brown. Serve warm; see if anyone can guess the special ingredient!

Day 14: Thursday 16th August

It was a fine breezy day, so I seized the opportunity to do masses of washing. We'd found Bruce's hat, lost some time before, lying filthy in a car park by the old chapel in Eoligarry. That had a pre-soak and two washes, from which it came out good as new. I found a couple of cookery books in the library that sounded like my kind of thing, and promised myself a nice evening going through them. It was a good time to read since the internet was playing up and so slow it wasn't worth looking at. The technician who arrived to look into our problem spent over three hours with us, after which we had high hopes of joining the twenty-first century once more. In the interim, I baked with my can for the day. I know Polish people love making plum cake, so what's so different about using prunes?

I was glad this recipe lived up to my expectations as I begrudge using 3 eggs in anything non-savoury. The broadband engineer inhaled his slice, and a visitor tasted it and thought it was chocolate and cinnamon cake, which is a result! A prune is just a concentrated sweet plum, after all, even if the Poles use fresh plums in their baking.

PRUNE CAKE

300g sugar
240g flour
1 tsp baking soda
1 tsp mixed spice
1 tsp salt
240 ml vegetable oil
120 ml liquid from a can of prunes
180g drained, stoned prunes

3 eggs
1 tsp vanilla essence/extract

Grease a baking dish or cake tin of around 10 inches.
Pre-heat the oven to gas 4, 350F/180C.
Mix the first five ingredients together then beat in the rest.
Pour into the tin and put in the oven.
Check after 45 min. to see if a knife blade comes out clean when inserted into the middle of the cake. If not, leave it a bit longer and try again until it does.
Leave in the dish or tin until cool, then turn out. I left mine upside down to provide a nice flat surface, then spread it with a bit of leftover vanilla cupcake icing. Yum.

Day 15: Friday 17th August

I'd been chatting with our neighbour Travis about Nigel Slater's simple suppers: a good premise from a chef unafraid of using cans, but since he has the option of nipping out to a deli in Hoxton or somewhere to grab ingredients for his spur-of-the-moment dish, I don't think he's much practical help for us here. I've looked at his 'kitchen diaries' books, and although the dishes sound wonderful from the comfort of my armchair, we'd struggle to get hold of the many things needed for the makings of them.

More everyday makings, though, we have plenty of: I'd got all kinds of cans of peas stashed away awaiting their fate, and one such came up for today. The freezers were *still* out of order in the Co-op, thanks to a fateful power outage, I was told. Since we get dozens of power cuts all year round, but especially in the windy winter months when the lines blow down, this doesn't augur well for the brand new state-of-the-art cabinet freezers installed just a few weeks ago. Anyway, this recipe is usually made with frozen peas, left accidentally or purposely out of the freezer. Since we didn't have any, I made do with the humble canned marrowfat.

PEA GUACAMOLE

A can of very well-drained marrowfat peas (177g drained weight)
A small amount of crushed garlic
Black pepper to taste
Chopped chilli/ chilli powder if you like it

Coriander and mint leaves, fresh if you have them, or dried herbs if not
1 tsp of olive oil
1 tsp of lemon juice
1 tsp of thick yogurt or soured cream

Stir everything together, then blend with a stick blender if you have one, or mash with a fork or potato masher. If you have time, refrigerate the mix for an hour. The dip should be thick and creamy. If it's a bit runny, you could add a sachet of vegetable soup mix powder (Tesco Everyday Value veg. soup in a mug is 25p for 4 sachets, and the basis of many sauces and soups in our kitchen) and refrigerate for 4 hours. Or... just have it runny! Serve with crudités, crisps or tortilla chips.

Day 16: Saturday 18th August

Bruce was relieved to have a familiar main course of penne pasta in pesto with cheese for dinner. Dessert, however, was more unusual. I was determined to prepare a sweet course beyond the humdrum, which was the downfall of a young writer in a book I recently read. It's a great true story actually: 'Bleaker House' by Nell Stevens. She went to a remote island in the Falklands to isolate herself enough to write a novel, but didn't take enough food: just over a thousand calories per day in a place where more supplies would not be forthcoming until the spring. Desperate for sustenance, she discovered a forgotten tin of peaches left behind in the house she rented, and decided to heat them in the microwave with a precious Ferrero Rocher chocolate from her rations. She managed to ruin both the microwave and the food, leaving her more frustrated and hungry than before. She tells this and her other adventures in a very funny style, with a clever narrative that keeps you guessing. I won't spoil the ending: suffice to say she came back in one piece!

Hoping for a less disastrous dessert, I scoured the internet for ideas until I plumped for this concoction, which Bruce declared "probably the best rice pud pancakes I've ever had". Since they were the only ones either of us had ever tasted, competition was not too stiff. But I liked them: they were creamy, light and not too sweet.

RICE PUD PANCAKES

Mix a 400g **can of rice pudding** in a bowl with 2 beaten **eggs**, 150g **flour** and a tablespoon of **sugar**. Heat an oiled frying pan then drop the mixture in large spoonfuls into the pan. When the pancakes smell toasty, turn them over gently with a spatula to cook the other side. Serve immediately, piping hot, with a dollop of **jam** or a little **golden syrup** or **honey**.

Day 17: Sunday 19th August

A cuckoo perched on our fence today. Some of the young ones still haven't got the message that it's time to head off south, as in the old rhyme, 'in July, away I fly.' They're not cuckooing any more, and I'm not too anxious for them to leave anyway: many of our southern friends lament not seeing them since the habitat and food for the cuckoo and the birds they parasitise (their chosen host for the cuckoo's own eggs, such as the meadow pipit and reed warbler) has been destroyed by modern farming methods.

There was plenty of housework to do apart from cooking, so I just threw everything that was hanging around the fridge in with my can of the day, Tesco's beans with vegetarian sausages. It just needed a little something more…

I love cooking with wine, as the old gag goes. Sometimes I even put it in the food! Begrudgingly, I sacrificed half a glass of my bottle of Australian red to the cause. I just made the rest of the recipe up. The wine helped with that too.

"LES RESTES" SLOW COOKED FRENCH CASSEROLE IN WINE

1 can Tesco baked beans and vegetarian sausages, with 3 spoonfuls of the beans removed and set aside for another day
A good splash of wine
Half-centimetre slices from a courgette, quartered
A small onion, chopped
A large clove of garlic
4 mushrooms, chopped into large-ish chunks
A splash of oil

Leftover cooked penne pasta

Coriander and mint leaves to taste, chopped, or a teaspoon of dried herbs, or both

A medium carrot, grated, or other vegetables, cooked or raw, grated or finely chopped

Put a slow cooker on "low" with the beans and sausages and pasta in it, plus the wine, herbs and half a can-ful of water to rinse it out and add some cooking liquid. (If you haven't got a slow cooker, simmer a pan on the stove.)

Fry the onion gently in the oil, then add the mushrooms and courgette and fry for another 5 minutes, adding a bit more oil if needed. Stir in the garlic once the other ingredients are looking lightly cooked, and add the grated carrot. Turn off the heat but leave the pan in place while you give it a good stir, utilising the residual heat and coating everything well in the oil.

Add the fried ingredients to the slow cooker or simmering pan, leave the lid firmly on for at least an hour or so, then serve with crusty bread.

Day 18: Monday 20th August

So it's tinned carrots as Can of the Day. Yesterday, when I bought a single carrot (6p) in the supermarket, Bruce pointed out that we had a vegetable bed full of them, fresh and ready to pick. I felt guilty with my 6p carrot. So imagine how I felt when I landed that tin.

The beans I added to our dinner made me feel more virtuous, however: they contain magnesium for protein management in cells and are in general a Good Thing. This is another of those accommodating homes for leftovers that comes out as something new and delicious!

I named my dish in homage to A Girl Called Jack, whose "cooking on a bootstrap" recipes, as I've already mentioned, are great: easy, cheap and quick. She has a dish called "tin bolognese" from which the following was born.

BOOTSTRAP BOLOGNESE PIE

1 tin of carrots, undrained
a dash of leftover red wine
a splash of oil
a few spoonfuls of leftover baked beans
3 or 4 sliced mushrooms
half a courgette, grated
leftover lentil loaf, 200g, crumbled (see Day 2), OR half a can of lentils and 100g breadcrumbs with 1 tbsp dried mixed herbs.
2 cloves of garlic, crushed
some snipped chives
a big squirt of tomato ketchup
a packet of ready-made puff pastry, cool from the fridge

Pre-heat the oven to gas 6, 400F/200C, and heat the oil in a frying pan. Fry the mushrooms till browned then add the garlic, stirring gently, for a minute or two more.

Take off the heat. In a mixing bowl, combine all the other ingredients, including the liquid from the carrots. The mixture shouldn't be too runny; if it is, add more breadcrumbs or lentil loaf.

Add the mushrooms and garlic, give it a gentle stir, and pour into a pie or flan dish.

Roll out a pastry lid and cut to fit, cutting a couple of vents in the top.

Place in the oven, checking after 30 min to see if the pastry is brown.

When it's browned, remove and serve with salad or spuds.

Day 19: Tuesday 21 August

Tales of hardship and deprivation in Bleaker House made me recall a dark tale written by an ex-GP on Barra, Rob Ewing. His novel focuses on children left alone here when a mystery illness wipes out the adults. They're reduced to scavenging while hoping for rescue or a means of escape. One day they find a couple of cans dropped behind the shelving of a looted shop. They're over the moon because they can be sure these foods are safe to eat, when all around them hunger and danger lurks. They try to be fair in sharing things out, but they're just kids after all... The book did very nicely and is surprisingly popular with visitors to the island in spite of the heavy subject matter. It certainly piques the imagination, and there's a note of hope at the end. Peter May's well-liked thrillers about the Hebrides are pretty dark as well, I suppose, though they too reach a satisfying conclusion.

Our tin of the day is peas again. A different sort: mini garden peas by Bonduelle, very sweet and delicious. I decided to make them into something to accompany the remains of yesterday's pie.

I browsed recipes for patties or fritters, including one claiming that peas were a "natural face lifting food". I'm not qualified to comment on that, but I created this very simple and tasty side dish, a sort of minty bubble and squeak that made us smile, thus lifting our facial muscles the easy way! You could add chives, cheese or any other leftover veg. and get away with it. Serve with ketchup or mayo, hot or cold. I pronounced my efforts a success.

PEA CROQUETTES

Chop a couple of **mint** leaves or add a little mint sauce to a cooked **potato**, peeled and mashed with plenty of **margarine**. Add **salt and pepper** to taste. Stir a well-drained **can of peas** into the mash, trying not to break them up too much. With floured hands, roll the mix into golf-ball sized lumps, then flatten into patties and press them into a plate of **breadcrumbs**. Fry in a little **oil**, turning after a couple of minutes. Quick, easy and cheap: my kind of dish!

Day 20: Wednesday 22nd August

It turns out to be the day of the pineapple. I was surprised to see instructions on the can explaining how to use its ring-pull to open it; doesn't everyone know that already? Should you be dissatisfied with this method of delivering the contents, there was a helpful postscript advising you to turn the can upside down to open it with a can opener if you preferred. Commendably thorough!

It made me wonder, though, why there aren't ring-pulls on all cans. Pet food seems always to have that easy-to-open function, yet many soups and other foods for humans don't, and plenty of people I know who are arthritic or less dextrous for other reasons struggle to use an opener.

The Internet has the answer, of course. The editor of The Canner magazine (I'd never heard of it either) says that the ring-pull can is a bit more expensive, so is used on products people are willing to pay a premium on: things that are a luxury already. She says market research has shown, though, that UK consumers would be willing to pay slightly more for added convenience. We currently have 22% of our food cans, including pet food, fitted with ring-pull tops, but the number is expected to increase. Recently, HP Baked Beans changed over to Easy Open Ends, with more brands sure to follow.

On YouTube, I watched 'the David Attenborough of engineering', Bill Hammack from the University of Illinois, explaining how and why cans are made as they are and found myself rapt: he has a delightful delivery and a clear and accessible way of explaining things. Basically, expensive aluminium is tough yet malleable enough to handle the force exerted on a ring-pull but the cheaper metals, tin-plated steel or plain steel, aren't. So you can fit an aluminium lid on a tin can or make the whole thing from aluminium, but both options are dearer. In the 1960s the ring-pull was introduced for cans of carbonated drink, but when opened the ring-pull came away from the body of the can, damaging the environment and harming wildlife. An ingenious design was developed which kept the ring attached, as Bill explains.

For people who have trouble with both ring-pulls and can openers, there's always an electric opener, and for those without either, the Internet has many crazy hacks to help you! See the References section for links to some surprising videos.

Trawling the WorldWideWeb once more, I sought a recipe to showcase pineapple rings in syrup. I could have made battered pineapple rings or a Hawaiian pizza. Instead, I decided to do this creation of my own as a kind of jelly mould, since I'd had a lemon flavour vegetarian jelly sachet in the cupboard for at least a year. I went completely off-piste, with a passing nod at Dad's Army. Private Godfrey's sister Dolly was always ready to serve up a pineapple upside-down cake!

PINEAPPLE PUD

I put a **pineapple ring** in the bottom of a small glass dessert dish, mixed the **jelly sachet** with a quarter of the recommended pint of hot water, then stirred in a bit of **soft cheese** and a splash of **pineapple juice** from the can. Since the jelly mix was still much stronger than usual, I expected it to set firmly in the dish so I could turn it out like an upside-down sponge cake. I prepared it early in the day, and at lunchtime, four hours later, I wobbled it eagerly. It was still stubbornly un-set. We ate some regardless with a bit of yogurt on the side, but there was no denying it wasn't as expected: it had a texture a bit like semolina pudding. A Fail with a capital F!

There's nothing like a failure to focus the mind: they say the (wo)man who never made a mistake never made anything. So from the same ingredients the very next day came **<u>PIÑA COLADA</u>**.

Day 21: Thursday 23rd August

I woke to a flash of inspiration. Piña colada is fairly similar ingredients-wise to the pudding I made yesterday, isn't it? Sort of: it's coconut cream instead of soft cheese, with some white rum and lime juice added. What about if I added some Aldi peach liqueur to the passed-over pud and whizzed it all up together? It's clear, like white rum, with a fruity smell and taste. Plus there'd be a citrus edge from the un-set jelly mix. What could possibly go wrong?

PIÑA COLADA

That evening, into the blender cup went the rest of the **pineapple pud**, along with the **pineapple juice** from the can, a little cold **water** to rinse it out and a few **mint** leaves. I applied the stick blender and poured the result into two glasses, then stirred a good measure of **peach schnapps** into each. Just because I could, I put a torn mint leaf over the rim of each glass as a garnish. I wasn't adding ice as the weather was chilly enough: strong northerly winds and lashing rain outside. Yes, in August.
That cocktail banished the monsoon blues. Our neighbour Rosanne called and was invited to try a drink of which she said she had many happy memories. Having dutifully tasted and rejected my version, opting for a glass of white wine instead, we had a nice nibbles and drinks hour: always my favourite combination. Bruce had had quite enough pineapple already and stuck to his usual cider. My second cocktail made me even happier. Hooray! From an epic fail she brings forth a roaring success! (Okay, that may be the drink talking.)

Rosanne had come bearing falafel balls and stuffed mini peppers, plus some home-made tahini. I produced crisps and was considering making some kind of spicy dip with our remaining soft cheese when I remembered we still had pineapple to use up. Jamie Oliver made a recipe a bit like the one below, but with onions and limes, and both green and red chillies. I just had one red chilli on my plant on the window-sill, so I sacrificed it to the cause, and created my version:

PINEAPPLE SALSA

Tinned pineapple, chopped into small chunks
Fresh mint leaves
Fresh chilli, chopped, to taste, or chilli powder
Fresh or dried coriander leaves
A dash of olive oil
Stir everything together, leave to assimilate the flavours if you have time, then serve with crisps, or as a novel topping for a baked potato and cheese.

The tin for today was actually spaghetti rings, or spaghetti-o's as Americans dub them. My heart sank at the sight of this tiresome nursery food. No vitamins there then. I looked on YouTube for inspiration and my heart sank further. There was some misguided soul setting a doughnut-shaped jelly mould containing the spaghetti rings, with mini frankfurters in the centre. Ugh. At least her jelly set, though. Another unusual fellow froze the can's contents in two square plastic containers, whereupon he battered and deep fried the frozen slabs, eating them like burgers with cheese.

Then I saw a short clip of a woman cutting into a hot, cheesy, juicy-looking pizza with spaghetti rings on top. That actually didn't look too bad. I usually serve pizza with coleslaw and some kind of salad, so my mission was coming together.

SPAGHETTI HOOP PIZZA

Open your **can of spaghetti hoops**. Drain off some of the tomato sauce so the spaghetti isn't too sloppy, reserving the sauce to put into a soup or gravy another time. Pre-heat the oven to gas 6, 400F/200C. Take 280ml of **warm water** (not too hot) and stir in 2½ tsp of quick-acting yeast. Put 400g **flour** into a mixing bowl and stir in a pinch of **salt**. Pour the yeast mixture into the flour and add a dash of **oil**. Knead this mixture for 5 min, then put the ball of dough in the mixing bowl in a warm place, with a tea-towel or plastic bag over the top. I usually put it on the stovetop when the oven is on. After the dough has doubled in size, about 20 min later, roll it out on a floured surface into a big circle. Place on a baking tray or sheet. Squirt a bit of **ketchup** around the edge of the pizza and spread it around the rim with the back of a spoon. Pour the can of spaghetti rings into the centre of the disc and spread out with the spoon. Sprinkle some dried **mixed herbs** onto the pizza. Cover the spaghetti rings with **grated cheese**. I had some mixed red and white cheddar and used that. (You could add leftover fried veg. on top of the cheese: courgettes, peppers, mushrooms or onion rings, for instance, but I left mine plain.) Bake in the top of the oven, checking after 15 min to see how it's doing. The cheese should be toasted and bubbling. Serve with a bit of salad or home-made coleslaw; mine was grated carrot, courgette and onion with mayo.

Day 22: Friday 24th August

We had another full-on session at the polytunnels although I was nursing a bad back from reaching too far when painting our bathroom walls. We took cuttings and potted them to grow on over the winter, weeded and harvested, then took freshly-picked produce to the community shop in Castlebay to put on sale. At last we had some toast as a token late lunch, then I opened today's can. It made these two complementary dishes:

SWEETCORN CORNBREAD

185g drained tinned sweetcorn from a 340g can, with the liquid from the can reserved
300g flour
100g porridge oats
55g sugar
a pinch of salt
1 egg, beaten
55g oil
Pre-heat the oven to gas 6, 400F/200C.
Beat together all the ingredients except the sweetcorn. The mix should be like a creamy cake batter, so add the liquid from the tin, then a little cold water, as needed until it reaches a consistency that drops slowly from a spoon.
Stir in the sweetcorn and pour the mix into a greased baking dish of any shape, but big enough for the mix to be no more than 4cm deep.
Bake for around 20 min, testing the middle until a skewer or sharp knife comes out clean. The top of the cornbread should be golden and the texture springy to the touch.

Serve with soup, or warm, buttered, with cheese.

EASY CREAMY SWEETCORN SOUP

In a non-stick saucepan, fry a small finely chopped **onion** in a little **oil**. Add some crushed **garlic** once the onion is transparent, stir it in, then add a peeled diced **cooked potato**. Add 50g of **sweetcorn**. Stir everything together then take the pan off the heat. Make up half a litre of **vegetable stock** from a cube or powder and pour it in. Use a stick blender to blend everything to a smooth consistency, or use a food processor or potato masher if you don't have a stick blender. Stir in 50g whole **sweetcorn** kernels and when ready to serve bring the soup just to the brink of boiling.

Day 23: Saturday 25th August

I drew condensed mushroom soup today. In the '70s it would have been in vol-au-vents before you could say Babycham, but I never really liked them. I'm not sure anyone did! Those other retro nibbles straight from a tin, pineapple chunks with cheese on a cocktail stick, didn't do it for me either: I'd rather have had the cheese on its own. You could get nuts in a tin back then, I remember. Apparently they're still sold at Christmas, but I haven't seen them for ages! Never mind the party snacks, I had a yen to do something more warming and hearty with my tin.

When we first moved into our little house here, our closest neighbours invited us to dinner almost exactly on this date three years ago. They're vegetarians too. They'd made a truly delicious home-made stroganoff with creamy mashed potato and we enjoyed our evening getting to know each other. Back home late that night, I recalled how in the Czech Republic in the days when I taught there, eating – and drinking – out was our chief entertainment. Stag and hen parties hadn't descended en masse on Prague, and there were some delightful places to stay that even teachers could afford. In my small town down the railway line from the capital, like Barra, there were few places to go out at night, but we always had a lot of fun. Stroganoff, served up seemingly everywhere I went, always brings back memories of those crazy times.

CAN-DO MUSHROOM STROGANOFF

Fry a **red onion** in a generous splash of **oil**. Add a crushed **clove of garlic** after a couple of minutes, with around 200g of chunkily cut **mushrooms**. Stir continuously as the ingredients fry, then add a good teaspoon of **paprika** and some chopped **chilli** if you like. Open **a can of condensed mushroom soup** and pour it over the top of the fried vegetables. Rinse the residue from the can with half a canful of warm water and add that too. Bring up to bubbling point then serve with rice or mashed potato.

Day 24: Sunday 26th August

A mysterious can appeared on the doorstep while we were out. We conferred on who could have brought us such a gift, and both came to the same conclusion: one of our can-party guests had come up with something else for us to try. It was un-labelled so as random a surprise as a can chosen by Scrabble letter. Later investigations proved that we were right about whodunnit: Clara had found it at the back of the cupboard and thought we were the perfect recipients. We decided to open it the very next day.

We'd never worried about the date printed on a can; before use-by dates even existed, our forefathers believed that they lasted forever. I thought I'd better find out whether they were correct.

Alan Aragon of Men's Health magazine wrote a piece about different food types and how long you can trust them after the expiry date. This is what he had to say about canned food: "Most expiration dates on foods in cans range from 1 to 4 years – but keep the food in a cool, dark place and the cans undented and in good condition, and you can likely safely double that shelf life from 3 to up to 6 years."

Back in the 1800s when the process was new, lead was used in canning, and the seals were not always perfect on cans. There has been speculation that Sir John Franklin's 1845 expedition to find the North-West Passage across the Canadian Arctic failed partly due to this: deadly concentrations of lead were found in team members' remains, although the lead piping on the ship could have been to blame. Since tinned food was an expensive luxury back then, it would have been mainly eaten by the officers who were supposed to be in charge, so their mental and physical decline compounded by scurvy and spoiled food is thought to have brought disaster to the whole party.

In the last century or so food technology has come a long way and deterioration or contamination in food is properly understood and can be prevented. The McGill University office for Science and Society in Quebec talks a lot of sense: "The canning process is very effective and cans which were produced over a hundred years ago have been opened and eaten. Problems arise if there is a defect in the can or if the heating isn't done properly. One giveaway is a bulging can. Bacterial activity produces gas and any can that bulges should be thrown away. Dented cans are a different story. The concern here is that denting puts strain on the metal and microscopic cracks may develop. The sterility is then lost and microbes and molds can enter. The risk is very small because usually dents do not produce holes. Dented cans do not necessarily have to be thrown out but their contents should be boiled to kill any microbes and destroy any toxin that could have been produced by the Clostridium botulinum bacteria."

That's the bacterium that produces botulism, but as they say, the risk is very low. If you've seen the 1989 film Dead Calm, in which Nicole Kidman gets chased round and round a sailing ship by a murderer, you'll know he blames the deaths of all his shipmates on botulism from a can. Nicole should have taken that with a pinch of salt! It's a creepy film with a farcical ending, if you're at a loose end one winter's night.

For this chilly late summer's evening, we had one of those lovely leftover situations, with the addition of a nice can of kidney beans today to give it some protein-packed oomph.

YOU MUST BE KIDNEY! CHEAT'S PASTA BAKE

Take some leftover **stroganoff or any kind of thick vegetable soup**, half a can of **red kidney beans**, and some **cooked pasta**. Pre-heat your grill. Stir the ingredients together with a heaped teaspoonful of **mixed herbs**, put in a microwaveable dish and heat until piping hot. Pour carefully into a Pyrex or metal dish and cover the surface with **grated cheese** (red and white cheese mixed together looks nice). Grill until browned and bubbling on top and serve immediately.

Day 25: Monday 27th August

While thinking about the dangers once associated with tinned food, it struck me that cooks often have a degree of prejudice towards it still. Did it earn its second-best reputation from those risky early days of canning, or from the bleak predictability of tinned food and what to do with it in wartime and beyond? I wondered if its labour-saving convenience was subject to suspicion by unenlightened misogynistic types back in the early post-war years. Many women had worked full-time during the long period of rationing and done their best to do most of the work at home as well, including the cooking. As everybody struggled to find a role once peace prevailed, was there an expectation that they should go back to being traditional housewives and spending the day slaving over a hot stove again? Those sexy American soldiers that many British women fancied were bigger and stronger thanks to superior food. I'm thinking there must have been a fair bit of jealousy and resentment around: an attitude that tried to push us back to what we were before, when in reality everything had changed. The world had come to Britain, and in the 1950s its produce increasingly came to us in cans.

The mystery tin from the doorstep revealed itself as artichoke hearts: Bruce was delighted! We could hardly wait to do our favourite luxury pasta dish with today's surprise.

HEARTY ARTY LINGUINE

Put a washed **egg** in its shell into a large saucepan with a little cold water. Bring to the boil while also boiling the kettle. Put some dry **linguine** into the same saucepan as the egg and fill the pan with boiling water to cover the pasta. Cook the pasta according to the pack instructions. Meanwhile, open a can of **artichoke hearts**, drain well and chop into large chunks. Smother in **olive oil** and plenty of **black pepper**. Remove the egg from the pan after it has boiled for 8 minutes and put it in a cup of cold water before shelling it and leaving it warm. Drain the pasta when cooked and put into a large bowl. Toss the oil and artichoke pieces through the linguine, sprinkle with **grated cheese** and arrange egg slices on top. Delicious!

Tip for warming bowls and plates: Drain the pasta water into your serving bowl and over the dishes you'll be using, spread out on the sink drainer. Leave the water to warm the crockery while you dress the pasta in the pan. Tip away the water and dry the dishes with a tea-towel just before you serve. Saves time, energy and hassle!

Day 26: Tuesday 28th August

The weather was wild. We chatted on Skype to Bruce's sister and mother in the evening and I asked them to tell me a letter of the alphabet each, to make a change from my picking them out from the trusty Scrabble bag. Jill chose K, which turned out to be mandarin oranges. Why, we wondered, do we only see mandarins, not tangerines or satsumas or clementines, in a tin?

Well, I looked up why: they're all mandarins of different kinds. Clementines are the smallest and reddest, tangerines bright orange with tougher skins and a sharper flavour, and satsumas a lighter colour with easier skin to peel but fragility issues due to that, which is why they're rarer in the supermarket. You learn something every day, I reflected as I tipped the little segments out of the can.

The day before, Travis and Erinn had gone away for a few days. They came to let us know with a parting gift of some cooked beetroot they hoped we could use. Could we add it to the citrus fruit, I wondered. I remembered something about beetroot in that old cookery book of Bruce's: dear old Linda McCartney had an elaborate recipe which could be simplified to make just the side dish we needed!

ORANGEY BEETROOT

Cube your **cooked beetroot**, then in a saucepan put **a can of mandarins** with their juice, a tablespoon of **white vinegar**, a tablespoon of **sugar**, 2 tablespoons of **cornflour**, 55g of **margarine** and a pinch of **mixed spice**. Bring to the boil, stirring all the time, then simmer for 5 minutes, stirring occasionally and adding a little more water if the sauce gets too thick. It will be a lovely glossy tangerine colour and the fruit segments will break down.

The liquid should be thick but pourable; add a little water if needed. Meanwhile, microwave the beetroot in a covered container, arrange on a warm serving dish then pour the fragrant sauce over it. The contrast of colours is gorgeous!

Day 27: Wednesday 29th August

I was still mulling over the origins of the prejudice against canned foods. Perhaps it could be due to concerns about keeping it fresh, and fears about little-understood risks associated with storing an opened can in the fridge. Acidic foods, such as today's can of chopped tomatoes, have a thin plastic lining inside to prevent the fruit acid allowing metals to leach into the food. It's not a big enough quantity of plastic to jeopardise recycling: labels, glue and old food are all burned off during the recycling process. The concern seems to be that once opened, the plastic in the can will contaminate the food if left for too long.

The Daily Mail didn't help when they churned out a scaremongering story about BPA, the plastic lining material used to protect the contents of both cans and Tetra-Pak style cartons. The reality is a lot less scary if you read the Michigan State University article: 'Worried about BPA in canned foods? Unless you're on a total canned food binge, you're probably okay.' Based on the conservative 'margin of exposure' determined by the FDA, and on the levels of BPA reported, a 70 kg person would have to consume over 14 cans of cream of mushroom soup, over 64 cans of green beans, or over nine cans of turkey gravy *per day* to be vulnerable to adverse health effects associated with exposure to BPA, they explain. The main reason not to store food in its can, inside or outside the fridge, is non-airtightness, which means the food dries out and loses flavour and texture.

It's not a snappy title but this 2015 study emphasised that making meals out of canned food can be good for you: 'Frequent Canned Food Use is Positively Associated with

Nutrient-Dense Food Group Consumption and Higher Nutrient Intakes in US Children and Adults.' This is according to the U.S. National Institutes of Health, who are probably a bit more responsible than the Daily Mail. The cheap price and storage potential of cans makes them a good option for people who are financially vulnerable: food banks nationwide make good use of canned goods.

My mother-in-law's choice of Scrabble letter led us to this can, at 34p one of the staples we get every week. I'd already bought some onion bhajis (reduced to 38p) for our dinner, to have with spicy potatoes and mixed green veg, so I decided to make the toms into a soup for lunch. While down at the shops in the morning, I grabbed a reduced-price pot of double cream. Everything else was in the cupboard at home.

CREAM OF TINNED TOMS SOUP

In a non-stick saucepan, fry a finely chopped **onion** in a little **oil**, until just transparent. Add a clove of crushed **garlic** and fry gently for a minute longer, stirring to make sure nothing browns or burns. Pour in the **tinned tomatoes**, then refill the tin with hot water and pour that in too. Sprinkle 2 tsp powdered **stock** or a stock cube into the pan and stir everything well. Put a lid on the pan and simmer for 10 minutes. Remove from the heat and blend with a stick blender, then sprinkle on some dried **basil** and **salt and pepper** to taste. Stir, adding 100ml of **cream** slowly to the soup. Serve immediately: enough for 2 generous bowlfuls.

Day 28: Thursday 30th August

After a lunch of leftover tomato soup blended with some leftover beetroot (what a lovely rich colour that makes: glad I didn't spill it down myself!) I opened the can of the day: one of the mystery ones from my can party. We'd been wildly curious about its contents as they sounded splashy when you shook the can, and the cryptic letters 'YJF' were printed on the top. If it was a manufacturer, it must be an obscure one. If it was some kind of retailer's code, it wasn't anything from Britain.

In breathless anticipation, I opened it up and peered into the mushroom-coloured contents. It smelt vaguely mushroomy too: a musty-ish aroma with a foetid tang. Was it field mushrooms? Can you even get them in a tin?

Poured out into a bowl, the chunks were larger and slightly fruitier-looking than I expected. There was the odd seed, and a firm core to the pyramid-shaped pieces, which spread into more fibrous formation at the wider end. It was a fruit, and it must be an enormous one. While travelling around India I remembered seeing whopping great yellowish fruits growing in Goa, but I didn't even know if they were edible at the time. What does a jackfruit look like inside? YJF? Yes! It had to be young jackfruit, used in savoury dishes and beloved of vegans, according to Google. There were some amazing recipes online and I was aglow with enthusiasm. You could prepare it like pulled pork, have it as a sort of barbecue sandwich filling, or make a spicy pie with a lot of texture and bite. Gina, who used to work in Sri Lanka, told us of big gatherings of family and friends there who would cook up and serve a massive jackfruit together as a coconut-flavoured curry.

When we'd been disappointed to find the curry restaurant was now closed, we'd talked about doing fajitas one evening as a spicy substitute. So in honour of our exciting new ingredient, I assembled the makings of dinner that night.

ALRIGHT JACKFRUIT FAJITAS

Fry an **onion** until soft in plenty of **oil**, add a clove of **garlic**, crushed, and stir in a pack of fajita **seasoning** mix. Drain the **jackfruit** and add to the pan. Stir well and cook on a low heat for 10 mins, stirring frequently to break up the pieces into a shredded texture. You could also add **kidney beans** to the jackfruit while cooking if desired.

Warm some flour **tortillas** in the microwave and serve the fajita filling with sliced **avocado**, **soured cream** or mayonnaise, spicy **salsa** and grated **cheese**. Everybody helps themselves to spoonfuls of whatever they fancy, rolled up in a warm tortilla.

Day 29: Friday 31st August

Bruce set off for work early as usual; I wasn't able to help him as a volunteer this time as I had to clean and set up the holiday cottage we take care of, ready for the next guests. It's the place we rented every autumn for years before we moved up to Barra, saving all our annual leave to spend as long as possible in the place we adored. We dreamed and schemed about living here every time we visited, and we're still on cloud nine now those dreams have at last come true.

I had loads of stuff to take to the cottage: a stack of nicely ironed bedding as well as cleaning equipment and towels. Clara fitted me in her car and dropped me at the cottage door, to my relief: there was a stiff south-southwesterly blowing and it would have been a struggle to get over the hill on foot. I washed and dried the used linens in record time, the rotary dryer threatening to take off at any moment, and zipped around cheerfully, hoovering, polishing and bed-making.

Tin of the day was beansprouts: I couldn't remember having them in a tin before, and there were certainly loads of them in there! I was doing a pizza that evening so I made up a crunchy little accompaniment for it, as well as a light and unusual soup to serve first.

SPICY BEANSPROUT SOUP

200g cooked potato, diced or mashed
around 150g of beansprouts from a 410g can, including the liquid from the can, with a few beansprouts set aside to garnish (reserve the remaining sprouts for another recipe)
a vegetable stock cube or enough stock powder for 500ml of liquid

enough hot water to re-fill the empty beansprout can
chilli powder to taste, or a chopped fresh chilli, Tabasco
sauce or similar

Pour the 150g of beansprouts and the can liquid into a
saucepan on a medium heat. Add a canful of hot water and
the stock powder or cube. Stir in the potato and seasoning,
adding more hot water if it seems too thick, and a little
coconut milk or cream if the flavour is too spicy. Stir till
piping hot then take off the heat and whiz up with a stick
blender. Serve garnished with the reserved beansprouts.

CRISP BEANSPROUT COLESLAW

Take a quarter of a can of **beansprouts** (50g) and drain
very well, then dry on kitchen towel. Chop into half-
centimetre lengths. Grate a small **carrot** and a piece of
courgette. Stir ingredients together in a heaped tablespoon
of mayonnaise or vegan **mayo** (see day 7) and serve
immediately.

Day 30: Saturday 1st September

At the long-anticipated Island Produce Show, I was helping to set things up. Other volunteers began logging entries early in the morning, spreading vegetables out for display and arranging crafts and artwork for maximum effect in Vatersay Hall. At last we took a brunch-break before the tense and secretive judging process commenced. It was very important indeed to be fair to all of those, from primary school kids to grandparents, who'd worked so hard to prepare for the competition. There was art, knitting, metalwork, baking, crafts, flower arrangements and of course a whole harvest festival of remarkable vegetables. I was reminded anew of how contrary I was being, opening cans every day when we had an abundance of beautiful fresh stuff outside the back door. Why was I even having tinned potatoes in the house when we'd Pink Fir Apple spuds, fresh and delicious, outside? We had perfectly formed carrots, crisp fresh lettuce, dew-drenched spinach and crunchy curly kale. Not all-year-round, sadly. Although I preserved what home-grown food I could, tins were a commodity that came into their own through the 'hungry gap'. Hopefully by next January, I'd be an expert in cuisine of the can. But in this fertile season Bruce had spent the evening before digging up our garden in the rain, washing muddy veg. and selecting the worthiest contenders for the competition. He'd grown some fine leeks, carrots, parsnips and spuds, and was rewarded with a pair of rosettes. The prize-giving ceremony was hectic and hilarious, with a couple of kids sporting more decorations on their shirts than a war veteran. To add to the melee, the rural housing scheme had a stand in the hall, giving away promotional bouncy balls which the kids promptly dropped, making the walk to the front of the hall to collect a prize more perilous than expected. It was like a bowling alley in there!

It was a long day but a fun one. When we'd finally finished checking all the beaches around Vatersay for rare birds, I popped into the Co-op for some Saturday night beer. There were also packs of Doritos, on their sell-by date, for the cracking price of 25p, so I grabbed four packs and went home to rustle up the Can of the Day into a very simple dish to go with our drinks.

<u>REFRIED BEAN DIP WITH HALLOUMI AND PEPPERS</u>

Open a tin of **refried beans** and put it into a microwaveable container. Cut some small chunks from coloured **peppers**, add a little chopped fresh or dried **coriander**, and include hot **chilli peppers** if desired. Dice a piece of **halloumi** into half-centimetre chunks and stir most of the cheese and peppers into the beans, keeping a few pieces of cheese and peppers aside. Cover the bowl (it will spit violently) and microwave until piping hot, giving it a stir after a minute or so and again when heated through. Leave to stand for another minute then transfer to a serving bowl. Sprinkle the reserved garnish on top and serve with tortilla chips.

Day 31: Sunday 2nd September

I'd signed up to have a go in an electric car, thanks to an awareness-raising green initiative. It was a BMW with weird doors that opened opposite ways in front and at the back, doing away with the pillar between front and back doors. It's supposed to offer more space for back seat passengers to get in and out, but also created a howling wind tunnel that would be problematic in our environment. The front door had to be opened before the back one would let you out. You also had to make sure the back door was closed before the front one, or they'd clash. These rear-hinged doors were once dubbed 'suicide doors' since if opened in a moving car, it would be forced wide open by the wind drag, endangering the passenger beside it.

Off we went in the spookily quiet car: it was very smooth and surprisingly powerful. The guy demonstrating it was keen to show me all the different dials and gauges indicating how little power I used as I drove, which was distracting enough for me almost to drift off the road at one point. But if you looked where you were going, it was a relaxing and comfortable experience, and we sped through the twelve-mile circuit of the island in style. Sadly, the two public charging points on Barra are currently unused and out of order, but you can always plug your car in at your house overnight. If you've got 35 grand to buy it with, of course. There are huge savings in fuel costs and road tax once you've bought it, at least for now, and no doubt they're the vehicles of the future. Having said that, I was intrigued to see how many of the fittings resembled a car with an internal combustion engine, although this one had no engine at all. There was a faux radiator grille, charging points at the rear corner where a petrol cap would have been, a parking brake button that lifted as though connected to a ratchet-style handbrake, and a bonnet that opened to reveal nothing to service apart from the screen-wash, which could more easily have been fitted inside the car. There seemed no reason to have an opening bonnet any more: just an aerodynamically rounded nose would surely do. The charging stations too were just like old-fashioned petrol pumps. Why? You might as well make them look like a carthorse's hay-net! Surely all you need is a unit on a wall, like a TV screen with a socket beneath it. In fact, a TV screen wouldn't be a bad idea: get a bit of advertising in to a captive audience while the promised 5-minute express charging goes ahead. Apart from my puzzlement about the styling, I was excited and enthusiastic about the car. It was much more responsive and nippy than I expected and if the price drops by a decimal point or two, we'll snap one up.

All of this activity left little time in the kitchen over the weekend. Luckily, my tin was a nice traditional one of sliced carrots (again), which I swiftly converted into a jolly nice lunch.

CARROT-CORIANDER SOUP FOR ONE

Fry an **onion** in a non-stick pan. Take it off the heat. Add a **tin of carrots** in their water, and a couple of teaspoons of dried or fresh chopped **coriander**. Mash together with a stick blender or potato masher. Return to the heat, stir in enough **hot water** from the kettle to reach a not-too-thin consistency, and add a little vegetable **stock** powder or **yeast extract** to taste. Allow to simmer for a couple of minutes. Serve with chunks of bread.

Day 32: Monday 3rd September

Bruce arrived at work to be greeted by a large box: someone had brought in a bird rescued from their cat. There's no vet here so he's the first port of call where injured or distressed birds are concerned. Expecting a mauled sparrow or battered blackbird, he was surprised to see a corncrake looking crossly up at him! It didn't seem to be damaged, so he carried it out to a nice scrubby area and it shot like a bullet into the nettles. Ground-nesting birds are in constant peril from people's pets everywhere, and in many cases they're endangered species already. That one, we hope, went on to migrate south successfully.

We had guests to meet at the holiday cottage who needed to be shown around and settled in. Since they weren't first-language English speakers, they might have needed a little more help; you can't expect them to read an instruction book of house notes in another language. Once the ferry made its ponderous way past our window in the evening (an hour late for unexplained reasons) we went over to wait for them. And wait. And wait. They never came. I left messages on their phone, I called Visitor Information in case they'd got lost and asked for help, I told the shop staff there were a couple of strays on the loose, then we left a note on the doorstep and went home. It was puzzling, and to this day we don't know what became of them.

It was late when we got back, so we had a collation of leftovers and topped them off with dessert using today's tin: coconut milk. This first effort was a roaring success and I'll make it again!

HOT TEACUP COCONUT PUDS

Beat an **egg** with 4 tablespoons of **coconut milk**, a quarter teaspoon of **vanilla essence**, 50g **sugar** and 40g **flour**. Add a pinch of **salt** and pour into a pair of microwaveable teacups (no metallic decoration or bone china!) making sure the mix is no more than halfway up the cup. Put one cup at a time into the microwave on full power, watching all the time. The sponge will rise above the rim; give it a few seconds more then pause and test the top for springiness. How long it takes to cook depends on your microwave's wattage. The pud will sink back a little but should be spongy right through when ready; repeat with the second one and serve in the cups with a spoonful of **jam** on the top. An easy retro treat reminiscent of nursery steamed puddings.

Sadly, the second recipe failed miserably. Worse, it was my own stupid fault. I'd looked online for recipes using coconut milk and found the one below with only three ingredients. Great, I thought: perfect for my lazy mode or time-poor moments; the cookies looked lovely in the pictures and had got rave reviews. I assumed, however, that shredded coconut was the same as desiccated, and found out too late that it isn't: shredded is moister, with longer strands that cling together better. It's easy to get in the U.S.A. but impossible to find on Barra! So the recipe below, using coconut milk from my can of the day plus desiccated coconut from the cupboard, fell apart. Literally. All that remained was a heap of toasted bits of coconut which now reside in the freezer, waiting for my next attempt at a korma. Below is what should happen – if you get hold of that special American coconut!

COCONUT COOKIES

180g *shredded* coconut
2 tblsp sugar
60ml coconut milk

Pre-heat the oven to gas 4, 350F/180C. Put a sheet of greaseproof paper onto a baking tray. Combine the ingredients until they form a sticky paste. Roll the mixture into 12 balls and press each one down, separate from the others, on the baking tray, to form a little disc shape. Bake for around 15 min. until browning at the edges. Cool on their tray for 10 min. before moving to a cooling rack. They'll keep in an airtight box for a few days - if you've made them properly!

Day 33: Tuesday 4th September

I've rarely hurt myself when opening cans; usually it's because of a defective tin-opener or a struggle with some improvisation, such as the feeble can opener attachment on a penknife when I'm camping. I managed it today though: I think the Can of the Day had a slightly dented rim. I'd used the tin-opener around the lid only to find a couple of tiny sections of lid hadn't been cut through. Running the opener over it again didn't help so I gingerly bent up the cut part of the lid, being careful not to touch the edge. I wanted to fold it back: half of the can would be open and I'd be able to get the contents out. However, as I bent the metal, one of the still-attached sections suddenly broke free, and the lid sprang up. The sharp edge sank into the base of my thumb, making a 1cm cut that bled like mad. I cursed and swore and crushed a tissue into my fist while emptying the can one-handed.

The Daily Telegraph reports that over 60 thousand people go to hospital every year after hurting themselves opening packaging, most commonly when opening cans of corned beef. In 2002 over 9,000 people wounded themselves in this way, though many, like me, presumably didn't think A&E was called for. The can needs to be that shape, by the way, with its razor-sharp edge, to get the chunk of meat out whole for slicing. All that fiddly business with a key: surely there has to be a better way? Other clumsy contenders for the Darwin Awards had actually cut their fingers off when using a knife to cut into a can.

I hadn't heard of many other can-related accidents: there was speculation that one fatal car crash in America was caused by a drinks can rolling under the brake pedal, and a chap I knew in Somerset had his prized vintage car damaged, though it was parked in the garage at the time. A shelf gave way under the 'last straw' of extra weight and dropped onto the car bonnet. Unfortunately there were a couple of dozen cans of paint on that shelf, and some of them opened up when it dropped. Ouch.

Help is at hand if a can does you a mischief, however: ambulance-chasing compensation websites such as 'first4lawyers' suggest that if you're injured by cans falling off supermarket shelves, you should get in touch. On a no-win, no-fee basis, naturally…

I'd bought a couple more cans to add to my collection during the day: more exciting ones than usual from the organic range at the community shop. At the same time I put my empties into the public skips. From here they're sure to be recycled properly, which seems less certain with plastic nowadays. I use the big skips not only to save the council collectors work and to avoid having extra bins in our garden, but also as a mnemonic: I see what I've just used up and replace it right away at the shops.

The can that cut me earlier wasn't the most exciting one ever, but I had something in mind for it, to make just enough for two. I watched my friend Fiona make this once for her table of eight guests, five of whom were unexpected: she's an amazingly resourceful entertainer and carried off the evening with her usual panache. Nobody leaves her house hungry, sober or unimpressed!

TUSCAN PAPPA AL POMODORO SOUP

A tin of tomatoes
Plenty of good quality olive oil
A clove of garlic

A few fresh basil leaves, or dried basil
4 thick slices of bread or a quarter of any stale rustic-style loaf
Salt and black pepper
200ml of vegetable stock

In plenty of olive oil in a medium-sized non-stick saucepan, gently fry the crushed garlic. Add the tomatoes, salt and pepper, plus a little water used to rinse out the can. Bring the pan up to the boil then simmer for half an hour, stirring occasionally. Turn off the heat, add torn basil or dried leaves, break up the bread and arrange it over the tomatoes. Pour the hot stock over the bread. Put a lid on the pan and leave it off the heat for half an hour. Just before serving, re-heat it gently, stirring but leaving bread chunks throughout the soup. Add a bit of boiling water if it seems too thick, but it should be very pulpy.
Serve in warm bowls with a drizzle more oil and extra black pepper.

Day 34: Wednesday 5th September

Today is International Day of Charity, proposed to the United Nations by Hungary in 2012 to coincide with the anniversary of Mother Teresa's death. It seemed like a good day to use my one non-vegetarian tin to make something that could be offered for a donation, or for free, in the community shop. It was a good day for soup. From almost noon and throughout the lunchtime period it rained heavily, so quite a few damp souls gathered to shelter inside. To my delight they ate the whole lot up, with one ravenous cyclist getting through three portions! Even more delightful was the total amount donated: over £46, for the RNLI. The lifeboats are a very apt cause for us to support on Barra as we all know people who serve as volunteers on them and often hear about emergencies close to home where their help is needed.

The recipe I used, with the quantities boosted to make around 20 cups, is loosely based on one from Nick Nairn of Ready Steady Cook.

<u>HAGGIS SOUP</u>

A generous quantity of oil
3 leeks, sliced
800g potato, peeled and diced
1 swede, peeled and diced
3.5 litres of vegetable stock
500g carrots, peeled and sliced
salt and black pepper
1 can haggis (vegetarian haggis if you prefer)

Heat the oil in your biggest pan. Fry the leeks then add the sliced haggis. Put in the other vegetables and stir to coat everything in the oil. Pour in the hot stock and stir well, breaking up the haggis. Simmer for half an hour at least, stirring from time to time. The soup will thicken due to the oatmeal in the haggis; add more stock if you think it's too thick, plus salt and pepper to taste. Leave to stand for 15 min. if possible, then stir well and serve.

Day 35: Thursday 6th September

We got up at 6.30 to go birding, enjoying the spectacle of a broad double rainbow over the highest hill on Barra. I perused the shelves in the supermarket, just in case there were any cans I hadn't noticed. There was Azera coffee in a can, or beer, or such ready-made drinks as gin and tonic in a one-serve size. Okay, I could've added one of those drinks to a recipe, but I'd been hoping for unusual cans of food. On YouTube I'd seen unlikely canned foods from distant shores: peanut soup, corned mutton or sesame leaves in soy sauce, anyone? Then there was Coca-Cola and coffee – mixed – as a refreshing canned beverage. I wasn't tempted. I did try 'Sweat', widely sold in vending machines when I was in Japan, but I was looking for something with a bit more nutrition about it. I was thinking of one of our favourite scary DVDs, 28 Weeks Later, in which there has been a plague with few survivors. A group who've escaped the city go on a supermarket sweep in a desperate search for something with vitamins. You've guessed it: they find it in safe, uncontaminated cans. We see them surviving over pot-luck suppers, can by can. This chilling tale, you'll be glad to hear, ends on a high note for the refugees.

To use our can of the day, garden peas, we made one of our regular standby dinners, ready in under 15 minutes, piping hot and filling.

PEA PASTA

Quick and easy in just one pan! Wash the shell of a raw **egg** and put it in some cold **water** in a medium sized pan. Bring to the boil then add your chosen shape of **pasta**, adding more boiling water from the kettle if needed to cover. Fish the egg out with a spoon after 8 mins of boiling and put it in a cup of cold water. Drain a **can of garden peas** and add to the pasta pan for the final couple of minutes of cooking time of the pasta. Meanwhile, shell the egg. Put 3-4 tbsp red or green **pesto** in a pasta bowl with a squirt of **ketchup** and a dash of **oil**. Drain the pasta and peas and put in the bowl. Stir to cover in dressing. Sprinkle with **grated cheese**, then quarter the egg and put the quarters on top of the cheese. A satisfying and speedy supper.

Day 36: Friday 7th September

Our friend Ken was due to arrive from Fife on the ferry with a box for me: I'd sent him a shopping list of 21 cans which are unavailable here, to add to my collection. To my delight he also brought us some red wine to enjoy with our dinners!

Tin of the day was cashew nut gourmet paté, which Bruce was very pleased with. He spread it on brown toast in traditional style. I'd read that leftover pâté can be used to fill home-made ravioli or stirred into a white sauce to make a rich dressing for pasta, but there were never going to be any leftovers from this little can! Besides, my previous attempts at home-made pasta were stodgy, to say the least. I didn't want to spoil the tasty spread, and none of it went to waste.

Nellie Melba, the celebrated Victorian soprano, had no fewer than four dishes named after her by the French chef Auguste Escoffier, including the one I made. The others are Peach Melba, which is peaches, raspberry sauce and ice-cream, Melba Sauce, a fruit compote with raspberries and redcurrants, and Melba Garniture, a chicken dish with truffles and mushrooms stuffed into tomatoes and smothered in sauce. That last recipe was a new one on me, and really doesn't sound that great: it reminds me of The Simpsons when the waiter is asked for 'your finest food stuffed with your second finest' and he produces lobster stuffed with tacos! I experimented with the most straightforward of Escoffier's recipes, a posher kind of toast, and after a bit of fiddling, succeeded in making some dainty-looking slices (and a whole heap of failures for the birds!)

MELBA TOAST

Take a couple of pieces of **thick/medium sliced bread** and toast them lightly in a toaster. Meanwhile, heat the grill. Cut off the crusts once the toast is done and very carefully halve the slices of toast through the middle with a sharp knife (I used a small, finely serrated one) so you have four slices of the same size but thinner, each with a toasted and un-toasted side. Cut these four slices diagonally to make eight triangles and put them un-toasted side up under the grill, not too near the heat source. Watch them carefully as these thin slices will easily burn; allow them to toast gently and curl a little. Serve with pâté.

Day 37: Saturday 8th September

We were invited to an event called 'coast: how we see the sea'. A visiting interviewer wanted to get residents' views, so we went along to meet her. We talked about Scottish marine protected areas and were asked about what living in a coastal community means to us. We could express our thoughts by talking or drawing, so I did both, doodling as we chatted. The Hebridean chain of isles has 218,000 visitors per year, 85% of whom come here by ferry, so we have them to think about as well as ourselves. It was thought-provoking and a good way to consider the islands' future, inextricably linked as it is to the waters surrounding us.

The Screen Machine was in town: our very own mobile cinema folded out from the back of an HGV! Excitedly we queued to see Mission Impossible, which showed to a packed and enthusiastic crowd. It's so rare we got the chance to see a film, we simply couldn't miss it, and we weren't disappointed.

Before the film I got our dinner going. I'd bought a taco kit a few days before, so when chopped tomatoes came up as the day's tin, I knew just the recipe: a vegan meal using produce from our garden.

<u>VEGAN TACOS</u>

In a large pan, fry a sliced **onion** in plenty of oil, add sliced **chestnut mushrooms** and thin **courgette** slices and allow to cook gently. Take 2 peeled **carrots** and make them into fine slices with a vegetable peeler. Add to the other vegetables, stir and allow to cook for a couple of minutes more. From **a can of chopped tomatoes**, spoon out about half of the contents, without taking too much of the juice. Stir into the vegetable mix, saving the rest of the can for another recipe. Add the **seasoning** mix from your taco kit (Old El Paso brand is vegan) and allow to simmer for a couple of minutes. Turn off the heat and leave the pan to stand with a lid on it while you assemble the other components of your tacos, e.g. spicy salsa, guacamole, coleslaw made with vegan mayo (see Day 7) and shredded lettuce. Enjoy this generous contribution to your 5 a day in taco shells with a nice cold beer.

Day 38: Sunday 9th September

For the first time in ages, it wasn't raining, but windy instead. A high wind was a good thing as it kept the midges away, and they'd been particularly pesky of late. The bin-men put mesh hoods on and workmen everywhere swatted and struggled if they didn't have the same. All kinds of unguent are recommended against the little horrors, but there isn't a single one we've tried that really works. So you either stay indoors or you don a fetching head-net. The bites just wear you down otherwise, making concentration impossible.

Our tin was stuffed vine leaves, a rare treat sourced from the community shop. They were big, juicy and shiny, with a delicate lemony aroma emanating from the rice-based filling. I'd read that spinach, even the large sturdy leaves we have in our garden, wasn't tough enough to replace vine leaves in a home-made version of these delicious dolmades, reminiscent of my broke backpacking days sleeping on the beaches of the Greek isles. I resolved to experiment with lettuce or Russian kale, spearing the parcels together with a stick of uncooked spaghetti. But some other time: we needed to get outside and get on with the weekend!

We had plenty of vegetables to have with our dolmades, and I made a pouring sauce with the left-over chopped tomatoes from the day before. It went down very well.

HOT TOMATO SAUCE

In a wide pan, bring half a can of **chopped tomatoes** to the boil with 3 teaspoons of **sugar**, some **chilli powder** or fresh **chillies** to taste, and a dash of left-over red or white **wine** or **balsamic vinegar**. Stir then leave to simmer uncovered until reduced to a more concentrated sauce (10 minutes or so; tilt the pan now and then to see how it's thickening). This goes well with all rice dishes.

Day 39: Monday 10th September

I'd borrowed a litter-picking device to do a bit of cleaning up on the beaches and roads where we walk. This long stick with a grabber at the end is ideal for reaching over fences and into ditches to pick up rubbish without imperilling your health and safety! Reactions are varied and interesting from passers-by when they see me walking with my recycled plastic sacks, gloves and picker: some applaud my efforts, others say it's a waste of time, and then there are those who see litter as somehow inevitable. "Ah, the bins blow over in the wind, and everything ends up down the road", they say, sympathetically but dismissively, as if litter is preordained and we just have to live with it. Hmmm. If what I collected was from domestic bins, I'd expect to see the wrappers, jars and cans from the things that everybody buys to cook with. But on both beaches and roads, what I'm picking up is exclusively debris discarded by snackers, beer-drinkers and smokers. I filled three bags with sweetie wrappers, beer bottles, cigarette packets and crisp bags. I filled another sack with aluminium cans which I recycled, and they were all fizzy soft drinks, beer or cider. The worst sections of road or beach are those which are not overlooked by houses: litter-bugs toss bottles or cans down or fling them from their car windows, assuming it doesn't matter if nobody sees them do it.

Well, it does matter. We buy nine and a half *billion* aluminium drinks cans a year in the UK. That's an average of 340 cans per household: almost one every day. And if they were all recycled instead of thrown in with general waste or tossed onto the roadside, there'd be 14 million fewer dustbins' worth of landfill every year. Besides, aluminium is expensive, and it can be recycled straight back into other cans. Should you manage to collect 100 kilos of empty cans (about 38 bin-bags full) you could sell them to a recycling plant for 50-75p a kilo in the UK. Scotland has been offering discounts and money-back offers in trials dubbed 'Recycle and Reward' to try to address this issue.

We need to take responsibility for our environment. We shouldn't expect to be rewarded for doing it either: it's common sense! As I pottered along, filling up my bags, it was clear that the wrappers and containers I was collecting were all from unhealthy consumption choices. Have you ever seen a poster that says, 'if nobody sees you eating it, it doesn't contain any calories'? It's not funny really. All of those litterers were making poor lifestyle decisions: putting rubbish into their bodies as well as into the environment. But if you hide the evidence by throwing it onto the ground, nobody can prove a thing.

Who are you kidding here? Just because we watch celebrities from presidents to footballers getting away with appalling transgressions, do we expect to do the same? Kids are taking this example as the norm. This legacy we're leaving: it's going to come right back to bite us.

Today I'm opening my 39th steel can. All of them have been properly recycled so far. Guess how many aluminium drinks cans I've gathered from the roadside and recycled? Many, many more than that. I'm not asking you to thank me: just help a bit if you can!

The can the Scrabble letter points to is condensed cream of celery soup. With such a rampant vegetable garden to pick from, plus a few leftovers in the fridge to use up, tonight's recipe is another wayward brainchild of mine. The nice thing about this 'bake' is that it doesn't need the oven. That means it's quicker to achieve the same result as an oven-baked version, uses less fuel, and doesn't leave burnt-on food all around the rim of your serving dish for you to scrub off afterwards. Bruce's verdict: "tasty".

BEAN AND VEG TOASTY-TOP FAKE BAKE

Put some **olive oil** in a frying pan and add two bread slice's worth of **breadcrumbs**, white or brown, seeded or not, as you like. Fry while gently stirring until they're nicely toasted, then put aside. Next, in a saucepan, fry a couple of sliced **leeks** in a little oil. Add a chopped **red and green pepper** and stir gently. Thinly slice **two carrots** and add to the saucepan, then a few **broad beans**, half a dozen **sugar snap peas**, cut diagonally to show the peas in the pod, and some shredded **kale** and **spinach** leaves. If you have any leftover **pasta** or a couple of diced **cooked potatoes**, they can go in too. Cover the mixture with **a can of condensed soup** (mine was cream of celery) plus a canful of hot water to rinse it out. Bring to the boil and simmer for 10 mins. Meanwhile, turn on the grill and find a flameproof serving dish of the right size for your bake. Pour everything into the dish, top with the breadcrumbs, and cover them with a sprinkling of **cheese**. Put the dish under the grill until the cheese is toasty and bubbling. Serve with crusty bread.

Day 40: Tuesday 11th September

I was still wound up about all the litter I'd picked up the day before. I looked online to see how long it would take to break down if I just left it where it was. The answer, thanks to the U.S. National Park Service, was pretty depressing. I'd found all of the things on this list when litter-picking, including marker-buoys and nappies. Worse, some of them are usefully recyclable and others, such as polystyrene cups, plastic bags and fishing lines, can kill wildlife when mistakenly ingested.

I sometimes find more interesting things: I still have a Victorian sixpence and an old King George penny from Vatersay beach, plus modern coins, and occasionally notes, dropped from the pockets of picnickers. Then there was a sea-bean: a rare seed-pod from southern oceans, considered lucky by mariners everywhere as it always floats. An islander we know found a tracking device from a scientific project to study fish migration. She got a cash payment for sending it back to the university in Portugal!

Here's the degrading-time list:
Glass container: 1 million years
Monofilament fishing line: 600 years
Plastic drinks bottle: 450 years
Disposable nappy: 450 years
Aluminium can: 80-200 years
Foamed plastic buoy: 80 years
Foamed plastic cup: 50 years
Rubber boot sole: 50-80 years
Tin cans: 50 years
Leather: 50 years

Nylon fabric: 30-40 years
Plastic bag: 10-20 years
Cigarette butts: 1-5 years
Wool sock: 1-5 years
Plywood: 1-3 years
Waxed milk carton: 3 months
Apple core: 2 months

So if I generously give myself a future 30 years of lifespan, I'll be outlived by most of my possessions unless I recycle them properly. This makes me think twice about buying more stuff, and less inclined to pass by the tossed-aside litter I see every day while out walking. I want to leave our home in better shape than when I arrived.

We were entertaining in the evening: Ken, who had brought us the exciting canned groceries and wine, came round to catch up on all the news. Preparing to feed the three of us, I was hoping for an exotic canned ingredient to come up, but boringly I got marrowfat peas. I decided to transform them into something a little less humdrum, which turns a lovely autumnal colour thanks to the turmeric.

A RISOTTO LESS ORDINARY

250g bulgar wheat
a good dash of olive oil
a sliced courgette
a chopped red or yellow pepper
a medium carrot, thinly sliced

a sliced leek
2 cloves of garlic, crushed
a can of marrowfat peas, with their liquid
a litre of vegetable stock, made up with boiling water
a heaped teaspoon of turmeric
torn basil leaves

In a large non-stick pan heat some oil. Fry the courgette, pepper and carrot for about 3 mins then set the vegetables aside in another container.

Add a dash more oil to the pan and fry the leek for 2 min, then add the garlic. Fry for a further minute.

Stir the dry bulgar wheat thoroughly into the leeks, then add the can of peas with their liquid. Bring to simmering point then add some of the hot stock so it covers the ingredients in the pan. Stir in the turmeric.

Keep an eye on the pan for the next 20 minutes while chatting and drinking wine, adding stock as the wheat takes it up.

Taste the wheat to see if it's cooked, then when it's ready stir in the reserved vegetables and top with the basil leaves. Enjoy with wine and friends.

Day 41: Wednesday 12th September

It rained a lot and the wind was vicious: a pair of hurricanes were stalking us from across the Atlantic. In spite of that, we were out birding as usual, watching the spectacular waves crashing against the shore and the unperturbed long-tailed ducks bobbing and diving among them. Back home, Lee told me he'd just opened the un-labelled tin with the oriental characters on it that he'd taken home from our can party. It was residing in the fridge as he had no idea what the contents were, let alone how to prepare them! I popped in to take a look, and by prodding and sniffing worked out that it was braised tofu. I offered to make it into something for him to try, so that sorted out the can of the day for me.

TASTY TOFU STIR FRY

A can of braised tofu, well drained and cut into chunks
A little cornflour
A good dash of oil
One leek, sliced
A few sugar snap peas, cut diagonally
One red pepper, sliced
Some shredded cabbage
A handful of beansprouts
A little chilli oil

Sprinkle some cornflour on a plate. Coat the tofu in cornflour and drop into a hot oiled frying pan. Turn the chunks until they're golden brown on all sides. Take them out and set aside, then in the same pan fry the leek, sugar snap peas and red pepper, stirring occasionally, then for the last 2-3 minutes add the cabbage and beansprouts. Arrange the tofu on top of the vegetables, drizzle with chilli oil to taste and serve immediately with rice or noodles.

Day 42: Thursday 13th September

It was another wild day with high winds forecast again. With a couple of friends, Bruce and I had a soup lunch at the weekly café at the polytunnels. The volunteers had laboured with love over the ingredients: freshly picked celery and herbs, giant home-grown onions and garlic, gently simmered tomatoes or leeks straight from the vegetable plot. The air was perfumed with good food and filled with lively conversation as we were led to a table, far enough away from the Mother and Baby Group that we could hear ourselves talk! Both the tomato and basil and the leek and potato soups were delicious, the more so as we were sheltering cosily from such a rough day outside. I resolved to ask them for recipe ideas next time I needed inspiration for my can project.

I'd been using my can opener much more than usual: until the easy-open can is the norm, it's another thing to rattle in the cutlery drawer and to remember to take away on a camping trip. I'm sure there's a place for electric and wall-mounted openers, but mine is the bog-standard key-and-cutting-wheel type invented in 1925. Naturally, I keep a spare for emergencies! The Napoleonic soldiers stabbing their way into dinner with bayonets moved on in time to the soldering iron, which after sealing the cans could melt them open again. "Sweet Fanny Adams", meaning nothingness, is what army servicemen dubbed the unidentifiable finely chopped food in their tin cans: it had to be in small pieces to get it into a small opening before the can was sealed. The macabre origin of the name comes from a child murder victim in London whose body was chopped up and spread over a wide area.

After years of soldiering or soldering on, as mass-production extended the market for canned foods, my kind of opener at last made cans safe and quick to open. Strange to think that one day it may be extinct, in the Museum of Domestic Life alongside the mangle and the butter-churn.

I picked the tin of the day, an event which was reminiscent of the National Lottery to my mind. How sad is that! It was the first of the exciting cans from over the water, brought to us by Ken: 'Finest' tinned cherry tomatoes in tomato sauce. A recipe on Tesco's website suggested turning them into a baked feta cheese dish, which sounded lovely, but I didn't have any of the necessary ingredients and no hope of coming by harissa paste, preserved lemon paste or pomegranate seeds in the near future. So I made a lasagne instead: one of my go-to recipes whenever I had a chance to cook for friends in the USA.

CHERRY TOM LAVISH LASAGNE

A pack of lasagne sheets
Three sachets of instant vegetable mug soup, mushroom or pale vegetable (I used Tesco Everyday Value Soup in a Mug, 4 sachets for 25p).
A can of cherry tomatoes (mine were Tesco Finest, £1).
Dried or fresh mixed herbs
Leftover cooked vegetables, plus canned beans or frozen peas or frozen mixed veg.
Grated cheese

Into a wide-based saucepan, pour around 3cm of boiling water and add a splash of oil.

Place lasagne sheets one by one into the water, making sure each is covered in liquid. Allow to soak for 5 min.

Meanwhile, mix the tomatoes with the veg. Mine included fried mushrooms and red and green peppers, chopped parsley and the dried herbs I had in the cupboard.

Spread a third of the veg. mix in the bottom of a square or oblong dish that's about the right size for the amount of vegetable filling you've made.

Using a spatula or slice and a fork, carefully fish out enough lasagne sheets, one by one, to cover the veg.

Repeat with half the remaining vegetables, then more lasagne sheets. Soak another batch of lasagne as necessary: you can just re-heat the same oily water on the hob.

Make up the soup mix in a small bowl. Make it quite thick, then pour half of the soup over the lasagne sheets. Cover with another layer of lasagne, then the last of the veg, then the last of the soup mix.

Sprinkle with cheese, and when it's dinnertime, put the dish in the top of the oven at gas 4, 180C/350F, for 20 min or until the cheese is bubbling. You're only heating things up: it's pretty much all cooked before it goes into the oven. A hearty dish for bad weather.

Day 43: Friday 14th September

In a howling wind we fought our way up the beach, past the picked-clean remains of a recently beached whale, slick drifts of sea-wrack and the tractor ruts running out to the oyster beds. "There it is!" yelled Bruce above the gale.

Sure enough, tucked in among the seeded grasses on the dunes, a tiny bird was looking at up us curiously. It was unfazed by the two interlopers on its territory; before coming here, it may well have never seen humans before. The little Lapland Bunting was the first of the autumn's arrival of its kind, feeding on the nutritious oily seeds of its winter residence. We stood stock-still, or as still as the wind would permit us, while it pottered around, almost within touching distance. Its feathers were ruffled up as it turned this way and that, oblivious to the storm, and we privileged watchers forgot it too as we caught a glimpse into its private and enigmatic world.

Back at the house, I opened our can: taco mixed beans in a spicy sauce. For a two-minute hot lunch I made:

<u>HIGH PULSE RATE SOUP</u>

Put a can of **mixed beans in spicy sauce** into a pan and add 2-3 heaped tablespoons of **cooked red lentils**. Add a little **boiling water** to achieve a soup consistency, rinsing out the bean can to avoid waste. Heat until beginning to bubble. No further seasoning required: enjoy with hunks of bread.

Day 44: Saturday 15th September

The Macmillan coffee morning was in full swing. I joined the queue at the entrance, saying hellos, waving or passing the time of day with just about everyone: the world and his wife was out in force. A woman I'd met the previous week, a newcomer here, was behind me in the line, and she couldn't believe her eyes. "If I tried to do an event like this back home, I'd struggle to get anyone to turn out. But this is packed!" she marvelled.

Donations had come in from all quarters: many people had their signature item of baking which they loved to make and share, and the customers had their favourites too. There was an overwhelming amount of cake, and every table was already crowded with happily munching people, so I headed to the raffle table, then the win-a-bottle stall, virtuously bypassing the boxes and trays of take-home sweet goodies for sale. The small girl in front of me, to her mother's amazement, landed the ticket for the star prize: a litre of gin. There weren't just drinks as prizes, but all manner of foodstuffs and bottles of perfume and toiletries as well.

It was my turn. The stallholder's daughter fanned out a deck of cards and I made a show of choosing one, then we looked hopefully for its twin with a prize standing on it. Yes! I'd won something. And it was so apt: a can of Heinz beans. I bore them away with pride and made it past the cakes again on the way out.

The tin of the day was peas again. I'd got a reduced-price quiche in the supermarket too, so to accompany it, and to use the peas, I made up a quick and tasty recipe, a twist on the traditional comfort food served in every pub in Ireland with a bar menu.

CHAMPION BEAN CHAMP

Take a couple of medium-sized whole **potatoes** and microwave until soft (about 7 mins for 2 spuds, depending on their size) then allow to cool enough to handle. Peel off the skins and mash the spuds with a little **margarine** or oil. Gently stir in some **beans** of any kind and half a can of drained **marrowfat peas**. Press the mixture into a hot oiled frying pan, turning after a couple of minutes with a spatula so that the crispy brown underside is visible. Fry for a couple of minutes more then serve with **ketchup** or **brown sauce**.

Day 45: Sunday 16th September

The south of Britain was having warm and humid weather thanks to south-westerly winds as a trio of hurricanes swirled around the globe. It wasn't warm where we were, but it was damp all right: we hardly stepped out of the house without donning the waterproofs and wellies. I did some ironing and cleaning up while Bruce sat on a headland in the rain logging seabirds as they flew past. I plotted the fate of today's tin, vegetarian bolognese, while I worked. Spag bol was a bit dull, I thought, though Bruce enjoys it. I had baked beans going begging too, plus some lasagne sheets left over from the other day, and as I pressed pillowcases and folded towels my thoughts came together. There are no cannelloni tubes ready-made in the shops round here, but I had a cunning plan…

CAN CANNELLONI

10-12 lasagne sheets
a can of vegetarian bolognese
baked beans or other canned beans in sauce
2 sachets of instant soup mix (see Day 42)
a little grated cheese
a dash of oil

Cook the lasagne sheets in a wide pan of water with a little oil for 5-7 mins.
Meanwhile, mix the beans with the bolognese and make up the soup mix in a small jug, making it quite thick.
Carefully remove a sheet of lasagne and lay it in a greased square or oblong ovenproof dish.

Run a couple of spoonfuls of the bean-bolognese mixture along the middle of the length of the sheet, then pick up one long side with your fingers and roll it over so it tucks into the other side of the sheet, like you're making a Swiss roll.

Shuffle the roll to the edge of the dish and bring out another lasagne sheet.

Repeat the filling and rolling process, squashing the rolls side by side in the dish as you make them. They will help each other to hold together if firmly packed in.

When the dish is filled by a row of cannelloni, pour the soup mix over the middle of the tubes then sprinkle everything with cheese.

Bake at gas 4, 180C/350F, for 15 min. Enjoy with green veg.

Day 46: Monday 17th September

I dashed out of the house as I'd been promised a lift into Castlebay, only realising later that I'd forgotten to pick out the can of the day. As I went about my errands, paying a bill, taking library books back, catching up with a friend who'd been away, I picked up litter, especially cans. I crossed the street for a can rolling wretchedly in the gutter and realised with surprise that it was unopened. I squeezed it experimentally, as sometimes they're discarded because they have a pinprick hole that leaks and makes everything horribly sticky, but it was still firm and pressurised. Thoughtfully, I put it in my pocket and headed on to the shops. I'd asked what became of the dented cans in our supermarket: in big stores they have a shelf of damaged goods with a price reduction, since imperfect packaging won't stack up. I was told that it still got sold, with a few pence off at the till if the customer mentioned its defectiveness. Very sensible and less of a hassle for all concerned!

Dropping the empty cans I'd collected into the recycling bin, I considered my acquisition. This can had chosen *me*. I'd make it today's tin and find something to do with it: something to avoid wasting its 4 teaspoons of sugar, making its long journey from the Coca-Cola factory worthwhile.

I'd read that vegans and diet-conscious people, including those with food intolerances, replaced the eggs, milk or fat called for in sponge cake recipes or ready-prepared cake mixes with fizzy pop. It was seat-of-the-pants experimental cookery that appealed to my slapdash side: just make up the mix with enough liquid to resemble an everyday cake batter consistency, stick it in the oven and cross your fingers!

FANTA CAKE

Take **one packet of cake mix** (I used Wright's ginger cake mix because it was on special offer: 500g mix for £1.29). Open **a can of Fanta**. Measure out 260ml and add to the cake mix. (This replaces the combined amount of water and oil normally added to the cake mix: if your pack instructions call for added eggs, replace them with 45ml Fanta per egg; if there's milk or other liquid to be added, replace with the same amount of Fanta.) Beat the ingredients together. Pour the mix into a lined baking dish. I used a sheet of greased non-stick foil as a liner. Bake on gas 4, 350F/180C, for around 30 mins, keeping an eye on the cake and testing if it's done by seeing if a knife blade comes out clean when inserted into the middle. Let the cake cool in its dish, spread with **icing or buttercream** if liked, then slice. The cake was great: orangey and gingery, moist, and so easy!

Day 47: Tuesday 18th September

By the end of Monday it was raining in torrents. Bruce and I both came in soaked, stuffing wringing wet clothes straight into the washing machine. In the morning's sulky grey breeze, I dragged on my still-wet jacket, hung a load of laundry hopefully on the washing line, and headed out to the charity shop. You never know what you'll find there: it's full of surprises, from an automatic roaming floor mopper to a fancy-dress giraffe costume. I keep a wish-list of things unavailable on the island, such as shoes or boots for work, waterproofs or kitchen gadgets to play with (and probably return for someone else to try). There was a pasta-maker without instructions this time, but given my previous failures with home-made pasta I gave it a miss. Someone had brought in a bread-maker too, but we've got one and it's working fine. No purchases today then.

My random tin was green beans. I'd been thinking about pancake-style savouries for a while: in the past I'd done such things with eggs and milk, but I begrudge buying milk when we don't use it for hot drinks or anything else, or using eggs in an "invisible" way just to bind ingredients together. Encouraged by yesterday's success with the Fanta recipe, I went off-piste again and knocked up another experiment.

GREEN BEAN FRITTERS

Drain **a can of green beans**. Mix 200g of **flour** with half a teaspoon of **turmeric** and a pinch of **salt**. Beat in 180 ml **water**, bit by bit, to make a creamy batter. Stir in the beans. Heat a frying pan containing a good splash of **oil** and drop a dollop of mix into the pan using two spoons.

Repeat, making sure the fritters stay separate in the pan. Once they will slide freely, turn them over, adding more oil if needed, and fry for another couple of minutes. Serve hot, sprinkled with chopped chives, ketchup or Indian lime pickle.

Day 48: Wednesday 19th September

It was our fourth wedding anniversary: fruit and flowers were the gifts to give, or so I read. I looked again at my YouTube video about making a rose from an aluminium can: the guy doing it undoubtedly has fingers of steel. He does warn, "…be very careful not to cut yourself", but I really can't imagine managing not to! It's a good idea to recycle of course, and aluminium cans already consist of 70% recycled material. It's a thinner, more malleable container than a tin can, but I could do without an hour getting stitches down at the doctor's, today or any other day.

Luckily, my tin was cream of tomato soup, a fruit I could turn into a gift. I'd also found an unusual recipe to try, which was so simple it seemed almost too good to be true. So while Bruce made me a leek and potato soup using the freshest of ingredients straight from our garden, I created a loaf to accompany it. We followed that with our favourite pasta, tagliatelle, with red pesto and grilled Mediterranean vegetables. Oh, and a glass or two of red wine: grapes are a fruit too!

DELICIOUS RED SOUP BREAD

400g can cream of tomato soup
270g flour
A little water
Herbs, fresh or dried.

Pre-heat the oven to gas 4, 180C/350F. Put the flour and herbs in a bowl, mix in the can of soup and rinse out the tin with a little water. There should be just enough liquid to hold the ingredients together; add a bit more flour if necessary to make a firm dough. Put the dough into a small loaf tin, roll into a rustic baguette shape or make half a dozen rolls. Keep an eye on the bread as it bakes and test with a skewer or knife for done-ness. You can also make the loaf in a breadmaker on the "bake" setting, testing in the same way: in mine it took 55 minutes, but it may well vary.

This is a dense flavoursome loaf which looks amazing when sliced and grilled with a grated white cheddar cheese topping. Nobody will believe what it's made from!

Day 49: Thursday 20th September

The Hebrides International Film Festival was going well: two days of unusual and exciting films from around the globe, chosen to raise awareness of our environment and its diversity. It was held on Vatersay in their community hall, and on both days I hitched a lift out across the causeway through gale-force south-easterlies to help with the event. There were still a good few holidaymakers around, including those in camper-vans and on cycling tours who were only too glad to get out of the weather and inside four walls for a while. I was making tea and offering soups and snacks, while other volunteers sold tickets, collected feedback forms and provided local information. There's no mobile phone signal on Vatersay so people enquired about weather forecasts and ferry cancellations as well as the screenings. The Co-op was looking rather empty and forlorn as boats carrying supplies were delayed by the storms, but on the plus side, I got a couple of bargains before they went out of date. They'd be fine in the freezer for another time. We were entertaining a friend who'd reversed his diabetes on a low-carbohydrate diet, so I'd planned a menu that would keep him on track. My day's tin was red kidney beans in spicy sauce, so we had a zesty little starter and a few drained beans to add to the main course.

EASY BEAN DIP

Drain the spicy liquid from **a can of kidney beans in chilli sauce** into a bowl and add two tablespoonfuls of the beans. Mash with a fork, then stir in another tablespoonful of beans but leave them whole. Add a little **tomato purée** (or ketchup if you don't have any) and serve with crudités.

LOW CARB CAULI-BASED PIZZA

Pre-heat the oven to gas 6, 400F/200C.

Take a large **cauliflower**. Put the florets and the less woody part of the stalk, chopped into chunks, in a food processor and reduce them to pulp. Spread the pulp over the base of a large baking tray and bake for 15 minutes, then remove but leave the oven on. Cool the cauliflower pulp (stirring will help it to cool down) until it's okay to touch, then wrap the pulp in a clean tea towel. Squeeze out as much moisture as you can: I got a couple of cupfuls out of mine, wringing it out inside the cloth first one way then the other. Put the pulp in a mixing bowl and stir in a handful of any kind of **flour** (coconut or chickpea flours are much lower in carbs than wheat flour) and a teaspoon of **turmeric**. Add a teaspoon of **dried mixed herbs**, then stir in a **beaten egg**. Oil a clean baking tray and spread the mix on it, just under 1cm thick, to form your pizza base. Firm it down with the back of a spoon to help it to hold together. Put back in the oven for 10 min. Meanwhile, assemble the pizza topping ingredients. I used a small **tin of tomato purée** mixed with a tablespoon of **red pesto**, spread on the pizza base with the back of a spoon, some leftover fried **mushrooms** and some **tinned sweetcorn** and **tinned kidney beans,** all topped with plenty of **grated cheese**. Check the pizza base for firmness, baking for longer if it still needs firming up, then add the topping and return to the oven until the cheese is bubbling. Serve immediately with coleslaw on the side.

Day 50: Friday 21st September

To mark World Peace Day, an out-of-breath artist with a huge and weighty roller suitcase brought an installation over on the ferry to Barra for one day only. It was a huge collection of plywood model boats grouped together to form the shape of one bigger boat, entitled 'This Little Boat'. Colourfully and imaginatively decorated by people of all ages and many nationalities, they represented a coming-together to create something positive in a world where apprehensiveness about the future clouds our worldview. The exhibit had travelled to other countries: 'people-powered' rather than by using an engine. Preoccupied as I was by my food challenge, I told the artist, Kathryn Brown, tales I'd heard from people who'd done time in jail. A few weeks previously, there was a five-day hunger strike in Washington State Penitentiary, when a 'breakfast boat' replaced a traditional meal in the company of other inmates. This was a cardboard dish containing powdered milk, cereal and a breakfast bar, handed out the night before to be eaten in the cells. The protesters now get fresh porridge instead.

It's obvious that morale will rise and conduct improve when prisoners eat hot food with their peers. I've been told by insiders about the 'food boating' organised between British inmates: they form a club to buy or otherwise get hold of ingredients, cooking them up with amazing inventiveness to supplement the bland and stodgy prison menu. A can of condensed milk is reduced to make banoffee pie, tinned fruit can be brewed with sugar on prison radiators to make Pruno (jailhouse wine), and for the curry fan, tinned ingredients can be prepared in a kettle to make a balti. It seems the guards turn a blind eye to these potentially dangerous activities: I wonder if the food-boat clique's involvement and co-operation in something so absorbing actually makes them more tractable. I bet they enjoy their creativity and the illicit edge to their cooking as much as the meal itself.

For our dinner it was beans again: cannellinis this time. They weren't ones I'd tried before, but they sounded good. We still had some of yesterday's spicy can to use up, so I did one dish for lunch and another for dinner featuring versatile and beneficial beans. They're heart-healthy, a great source of protein, antioxidants, vitamins, minerals and fibre, low-fat and slow to digest, so they satisfy for longer. All this and good for the budget too!

CANNELLINI BEANY TOAST

This is the posh version of beans on toast. Take a **can of cannellini beans** and drain well. Mash them gently with a fork so they're just crushed but still recognisable. Add a little **crushed garlic**, a splash of **olive oil**, ground **black pepper** and some chopped fresh or dry **basil** to the beans. Take 4 thick slices of **crusty rustic bread** and spread them with some **tomato purée** (or pesto if you haven't got any) then sprinkle **salt**, black pepper and a little more oil over the bread. Put the bread under the grill until lightly toasted on top, then spread with the bean mixture and return to the grill for another minute or two until the beans are toasted but not burned. Enjoy with a glass of white wine for a special lunch.

LEFTOVER BEAN HOTCAKES

I was inspired to make these simple fritters when recalling the delights of Asian street food. Put 60g of **flour** in a mixing bowl. Add **salt, pepper** and chilli or **curry powder** to taste. Stir in up to half a can of **baked beans** in their sauce or any other canned beans; I used up our kidney beans in spicy sauce, without adding any extra spices. Add a little **water** if necessary to make a thick paste. Heat a greased frying pan and, using two spoons, drop dollops of the mix into the pan, far enough apart that they don't touch each other. When they will slide on the pan's surface, turn them and cook for a couple of minutes more. Eat while still hot, with your fingers.

Day 51: Saturday 22nd September

Plum tomatoes came up again from the big box in the hall. They'd definitely be one of the cans I'd take with me to a desert island (as opposed to a remote island of Lewisian gneiss and a Co-op, where we currently reside). Apart from their amazing versatility in sweet and savoury dishes, I'd try to grow tomato vines from the seeds. I've read online that they're killed by the high temperature in the canning process, but I'm sure that in the past I heard my uncle Albert tell tales of growing plum tomato plants from canned seeds when he was a prisoner of war. So as an experiment, I'm going to separate them out and dry them on kitchen paper, ready for the spring. In any case, removing the seeds from a tin of toms is a useful life skill: many people find they get stuck annoyingly between their teeth or they dislike their bitter taste and 'bitty' texture.

My Desert Island Cans, I decided, would be the following, in no particular order, but preferably in the biggest possible size of ring-pull opening tins! I'd have a Swiss army knife as my luxury item if the tins weren't easy-open cans. You can have eight pieces of music on the Radio 4 show, Desert Island Discs, so here are my eight cans instead:

ghee: (it's 112 calories per tablespoon, and I could fry my fish or greens in it)
refried beans
marrowfat peas
condensed cream of mushroom soup
baked beans
chickpeas

tinned tomatoes

a barrel of beer (let she who is without sin cast the first stone…)

TASTIER TINNED TOMATOES

Take a salad spinner, remove the lid and pour the tin of tomatoes into the mesh part inside the bowl. Break open the whole tomatoes with your fingers and use your fingertips to scoop out any seeds you can see, releasing them from inside the tomatoes but leaving the pulpy solids in the spinner. Put on the lid and spin the fruit. You'll be left with the fruit pieces, mostly seed-less, in the mesh, and the liquid containing the seeds in the bowl below. You can now pick out pieces of tomato skin and core, or any unappetising-looking blackened bits from the ends of the tomatoes, from the fruit at this point. Lift out the mesh with the tomato pieces in it and pour the liquid below through a strainer. Voilà! Re-mix the de-seeded liquid with the tomato chunks and you're ready to cook with purer fruit, as well as harvesting those seeds to experiment with for a potential future crop if you're feeling scientific...

There were still spicy beans remaining from a previous day's can to add to the tomatoes, so I used them up in an individual dish as a pleasing change from a lunchtime soup or sandwich.

SPICY LASAGNE IN A MUG FOR ONE

Cook two sheets of **lasagne** per person for seven minutes in a little water in a wide pan (a still-greasy used frying pan works well for this). Place the lasagne on a chopping board, take a large straight-sided microwaveable mug and use the rim of the mug to cut four circles of lasagne from the two sheets. Chop the remains of the lasagne sheets into small pieces and put these pieces in a bowl with half **a can of chopped tomatoes** per serving and some leftover **beans** or other finely chopped **cooked vegetables**. Add a dash of **chilli sauce**, such as Tabasco, and stir. Put around 3 tablespoons of the mix into the mug then place one of the lasagne circles on top. Repeat until the mug is almost filled, then put the last lasagne circle onto the filling and top with **grated cheese**. Stretch a piece of clingfilm tightly over the top of the mug and wrap around the sides, then microwave for around 2 minutes, watching to make sure the contents don't bubble over. Take out carefully and leave to stand for 2 minutes, then unwrap and eat straight from the mug with a fork. You can make this in advance, leave it cling-wrapped in the fridge and have it ready to microwave whenever you're hungry the next day.

Day 52: Sunday 23rd September

The Americans, I'd been reading, got to grips with cans early on in typical can-do style. As a commercial product, canned food goes back to the 1800s over there. Van Camp, a manufacturer still in business today, supplied beans under contract to the Union Army in 1861. The soldiers got a taste for canned food and liked its convenience. It was common in domestic menus by the early 20th century but was still more expensive than fresh goods, so it was a supplement rather than a replacement. It became more affordable in WWII thanks to full employment, but by then it was rationed. Post-war, it became hugely popular, and once supermarkets got going in the '50s and '60s, all this added time-saving and convenience meant that even the most traditional cooks began reluctantly to accept tins.

In the UK, condensed milk in the 1850s was many a family's introduction to canned food in the shops. By 1880 we imported 16 million pounds of canned meat a year, and by the late 19th century European households could sample entirely new foods imported from the U.S. and elsewhere. Fast-forward to the present, where despite alternatives such as cartons and pouches, food cans are used by British households at a rate of 680 per year on average, and Europe-wide, 20 billion food cans a year are sold, the same as in the USA. That's great news for the industry: we consumers just have to make sure we recycle all that useful metal!

I've drawn yet another can of peas today: we've got extra eggs and some milk to use up too as more people we know have gone on holiday and left us the perishables from their fridge. From those beginnings, this recipe wrote itself:

HALLOUMI AND PEA PASTRY-FREE FLAN

4 eggs
50 ml milk
a drained can of peas (ours were garden peas but
marrowfat are fine too)
a 225g pack of halloumi
4 tbsp of other chopped cooked vegetables, e.g. red
peppers or onions
black pepper

Pre-heat the oven to gas 7, 220C/425F, with a small
greased shallow baking dish inside on the top shelf as it
heats up.
Cut the halloumi into 6 slices and beat the eggs and milk
together.
Take out the hot dish and carefully arrange the halloumi in
the bottom. Put the other vegetables into the dish and
sprinkle with black pepper.
Pour the egg mixture over the vegetables and return to the
oven.
Cook for around 20 min. until firm and golden on top: it
will fluff up as it firms.
You could use Indian paneer or Greek feta instead of
halloumi, and of course the combinations of vegetables (or
olives, beans or finely chopped pasta) make this a speedy,
versatile and leftover-friendly dinner.

Day 53: Monday 24th September

I had plenty to do early in the morning: laundry with a rare chance to get it dry outside, recycling bins to put out and bring back for our place and the nearby houses before they blew away out into the bay, and emails for people to receive when they started work. It was wonderful to see the sun, and I wanted to make the most of the day.

I was especially excited, therefore, to open a ready meal in a can: a healthy vegetable balti. Being organic and vegan, it already had green qualifications, and canning must be one of the most eco-friendly food storage methods. Though energy is used to pre-cook the food, it's in a completely recyclable container that doesn't need to be frozen or refrigerated. It's got the longest, safest storage life in the grocery world: no weevils or vermin can get to it, but it's convenient for us to access and needs little heating or preparation time.

The balti smelt divine when I opened the can and I knew Bruce would adore it just as it was. So how could I complement this perfect dish? Well, how about extra vitamins, antioxidants and fibre without adding stodgy empty calories?

LOW CARB TASTY CAULIFLOWER RICE

1 large cauliflower
a good dash of oil
a small onion, finely chopped
1 clove garlic, crushed
1 tbsp turmeric
1 can of vegan balti or similar, to serve

Remove the cauliflower florets and the non-woody parts of the florets' stalks. Chop into smallish pieces and pulse in small batches in a food processor until the cauliflower resembles grains of rice.

Heat the oil in a large pan and cook the onion on a moderate heat until transparent. Add the garlic and stir.

Stir in the cauliflower and keep it moving in the pan for 5 min.

Sprinkle turmeric over the cauliflower and keep stir-frying for a couple more minutes.

Serve immediately with any dish that calls for rice, such as a curry.

Day 54: Tuesday 25th September

The wind was howling and the wind lashing down when I toiled over Heaval, the tallest hill on Barra, towards the supermarket. My bag was laden with cans and bottles to take to the municipal recycling bins, and there was litter to add to my load from the ditches along the way. Thankfully, a local stopped to pick me up before I got thoroughly soaked, and after my errands were done I sank into a comfortable library chair. The ferry was cancelled thanks to the weather and unlikely to sail the following day either. There wasn't much fresh food remaining in the shop but I picked up a couple of bargains: a wilting 'salad pack' of tomatoes with a whole lettuce and a cucumber for 40p plus a carton of mushrooms teetering on the brink of their sell-by date. Those, along with our own vegetables being thrashed by the weather in the garden, would keep us going until the next supplies turned up. It's alarming how fast the shelves can empty at times: pre-emptive buying accounts for part of the picture, but apart from that there are up to a thousand residents alongside an ever-increasing number of visitors to our isles, in those aisles! These mainly British guests are often well prepared for the conditions with waterproofs, guest-house reservations and flexible itineraries in case of transport delays, but we're regularly astounded by how many step off the boat at 6.30 in the evening without a bed booked for the night, let alone a packet of biscuits to keep the wolf from the door. Clothes are another issue: hats sell well to tourists in summer when they're unexpectedly feeling the cold and the thrift shop regularly gets shivering customers seeking wellies and extra layers. To compound the accommodation issue, the plane often runs when the boats can't, so in the high season there could easily be a couple of dozen without onward transport leaving their B&Bs to make way for those who've just flown in.

At this time of year, though, the kids are all back at school and the pressure on accommodation has eased. It's only a fraction of the locals who remain while others take their holidays, their workload lightened with the passing of the high season. I had a tin of root vegetable soup to make dinner with, and I decided to make a low-fat, high-fibre comfort food recipe that would keep hot even if the electricity failed.

<u>HEARTY HEART-HEALTHY SHEPHERD'S PIE</u>

1 can of root vegetable and turmeric soup
200g cauliflower or broccoli cut into small florets
1 small onion, grated using the cheese side of a box grater (the less cooked it is, the more benefit your heart is said to receive from the sulphur compounds it contains)
a courgette, grated
3 medium potatoes, whole, washed
a little skimmed or soya milk
stock powder or a stock cube
black pepper to taste

Put the 3 potatoes into the microwave and cook in their skins for around 8-9 minutes until soft. No need to prick the skins, just test them for done-ness now and then.

Meanwhile, put the soup in a pan with the grated vegetables, stir well and simmer for 5 min. In another lidded pan, cook the cauliflower or broccoli for 5 min. in about 3cm of boiling water. Turn off the heat and leave both pans on the stove with the lids on.

When the potatoes are done, let them stand for a couple of minutes then peel them carefully: they'll still be quite hot to handle. Keep the peel and mash the potatoes with seasoning and milk.

Make up around a cupful of stock with the still-hot water from the vegetable pan, add the potato peelings and blend with a stick blender to a smooth consistency. Stir into the vegetable mixture and add the cooked florets.

Pour the mix into a flameproof dish and cover with forkfuls of the mash, using the fork to spread and texture the surface. Put the dish under the grill until the top is nicely toasted.

Serve with salad and a nice glass of red wine.

Day 55: Wednesday 26th September

The ferry service was still disrupted and the rain was teeming. Nevertheless, we donned our waterproofs to walk along the wide white sands at Eoligarry, revelling in its emptiness after a summer invaded by the bucket-and-spade brigade. Today, a family of otters was bold enough to stay out in front of us on the rocks, whistling a high-pitched call to each other as they romped and swam.

Our neighbour Rosanne came to share a drink with us last night, bringing a deliciously unusual salad which we finished off at lunchtime. It was so good and authentic-tasting, I begged the recipe and adapted it to my own ends:

ROSANNE'S MIDDLE EASTERN TAHINI SALAD

Finely chop **half a red onion** and add a little **garlic crushed with salt**, the zest from **half a lemon** and a tablespoonful of lemon juice. Add 3 tablespoons of **tahini,** 3 tablespoons of **natural Greek-style yogurt** and a few leaves of **chopped mint**. Chop a **cucumber** and **4 ripe tomatoes** into chunks and combine with the tahini mixture. Toss everything together until coated in the dressing. Leave in the fridge for half an hour, sprinkle with **ground cumin** then serve with warm pitta bread.

Today's tin is custard. After a healthy couple of days, I was pleased to see the makings of a dessert, which would be quick, simple and seasonal if I added some of the Cumbrian apples given to us by a visiting couple last week.

EASY APPLE N' CUSTARD TARTLETS

Pre-heat the oven to gas 6, 200C/400F.Take a pack of **ready-made puff pastry** (mine was 425g) and roll out to 3mm thickness. Cut circles from the pastry using a wide cookie cutter or the rim of a mug, and press the circles firmly into a 12-hole Yorkshire pudding/muffin tin, making sure the discs are big enough to overlap the depressions in the tray. Spoon cold **custard** into each one, then sprinkle with a little ground **cinnamon or nutmeg**. Use a potato peeler to take the peel off two washed medium-sized **eating apples** and put the peel to one side. Grate the flesh of the two apples and spoon a little of the grated apple into the middle of each tartlet on top of the custard. Add a curl of apple peel to each one, standing it up on its edge as much as possible, and sprinkle a pinch of **granulated sugar** onto each curl. Bake for around 20 minutes until the pastry is golden and the apple curls are toasted. Leave to cool in the tray for 5 min then remove to eat warm straightaway or cold later. Serve with leftover custard, cream or ice-cream.

Day 56: Thursday 27th September

I plugged on faithfully with my litter-picking as I walked to the recycling bins once more. The 'take 3 for the sea' campaign, founded by a surfer, Tim Silverwood, warns that unless we act, by 2050 the amount of plastic floating around in our oceans will outweigh that of all the fish put together. What a horrifying thought! Furthermore, you don't have to throw your litter down at the seaside to add to the problem: 80% of it comes from a land-based source. Birds and marine animals ingest it or become entangled in it, and minute particles enter the food chain via the smallest organisms. All around the football pitch there were bottles, cans and sweetie wrappers, not to mention expensive clothes and shoes strewn around, soaking wet. Sportsmen and women are meant to be health-conscious people. What's the example for the schoolchildren who come to watch the games? What sort of a future are we encouraging here? It reminded me of the old song: 'he's football crazy, he's football mad, and football it has taken away the wee bit o' sense he had...'

Plenty of the litter is non-recyclable, such as the packets for the crisps Gary Lineker has for so long endorsed. I'd saved these up and was sending each one back to the company's Freepost address in one of my carefully recycled envelopes, as part of the campaign for fully recyclable packaging. I just don't want to see it all over our beautiful island, and whenever I see the face of the nice guy who mows the football pitch as he trudges around picking up stuff thrown all over it before he can do his job, it firms my resolve.

The weather was still abominable, and to add insult to injury the Scottish mainland was enjoying another lovely day. We'd been promised one but it didn't seem to be happening, at least by the time I squelched up to my computer screen with soggy feet. The ferry departed on schedule, though, for the first time in a while, so things were looking up. In the interim I dug a pack of vegetable samosas out of the freezer to accompany the tin for today: pineapple rings.

TAKEAWAY STYLE PINEAPPLE SWEET N' SOUR SAUCE

From a small **can of pineapple chunks or rings**, measure out 50ml of the liquid from the can. Mix the juice with 100ml **cold water**, 50ml **wine vinegar** (red or white), 2 tablespoons of **tomato ketchup** and 3 tablespoons of **sugar**. Put everything in a pan and heat gently, stirring frequently. Meanwhile, mix 2 tablespoons of **cornflour** with a little water in a cup to make a thin paste. Once the liquid on the stove is bubbling, stir in the cornflour and keep stirring as the sauce thickens. For that authentic Chinese takeaway appearance, add some of the pineapple chunks and a little vegan **red colouring**. Serve immediately over noodles or stir-fry.

Day 57: Friday 28th September

It was a red-letter day: the bank won't be closing in January after all! Sixty-two branches were to be closed by RBS, and for Barra, having no other bank branch and a boat ride as well as a road journey to the next nearest one, we would have been struggling without it. Online banking isn't a substitute, given our unreliable internet and mobile phone services. Tobermory and Mallaig, isles suggested by the bank as alternative places for Barra people to go to a cashpoint, are a two-day journey away! I'm sure it would be a pleasant excursion, but honestly… Common sense has prevailed and our friends and neighbours joined us in a toast to that.

In a scene reminiscent of The Vicar of Dibley when Letitia Cropley alarms people with her unorthodox baking ingredients, today I made a Pea Cake. Why not, I reasoned. Courgettes are legitimately incorporated in sweet dishes, and so are carrots. Besides, I'd got some bargain eggs that worked out at less than 4p apiece. Perhaps I should call it 4p cake! Anyway, it was a different, sweeter way to use my can, and the resulting confection wasn't really green, just slightly tinged in a way that suggested it might glow in the dark…

SWEET SURPRISE PEA CAKE

177g drained peas from one can, blended to a puree
100g margarine
75g sugar
3 eggs, beaten
1 tsp vanilla extract

1 tsp almond essence
1 tablespoon lemon juice
125g flour
A pinch of salt

Pre-heat the oven to gas 4, 350F/180C.
Cream the margarine and sugar, add the peas and eggs then the liquid flavourings.
Beat in the flour and salt, adding more flour if needed to achieve a batter of a dropping consistency.
Pour the mixture into a greased loaf tin.
Bake for around 40 minutes till springy to the touch. When cooled, add vanilla icing or buttercream if you wish. Get people to guess the secret ingredient!

Day 58: Saturday 29th September

Our bird-watching friends arrived today from mainland Scotland: six of them will be combing the bushes and walking the shores, rain or shine for the next few weeks, hoping that rarities from east or west will be grounded for a feed and a rest on their migratory journeys. We had two birders over in the evening, chatting and catching up as we looked out onto the windswept bay from our dining table. In their honour, to keep yesterday's pea cake company I made two more cakes featuring the can that came up for today: carrots again. Nobody guessed that there were vegetables concealed in any one of my three offerings; in the film Forrest Gump, the eponymous hero says he and his schoolfriend are 'like peas and carrots' since they're always to be found alongside each other. That seems to work for baking too: perhaps I'll try both in one cake one of these days.

CANNED CARROT CAKE

1 can of drained carrots, mashed with a fork or stick blender
100g margarine
200g sugar
125g flour
1 tsp bicarbonate of soda
a pinch of salt
1 tsp mixed spice
2 eggs
Pre-heat the oven to gas 4, 180C/350F.

Rub the margarine into the flour mixed with the bicarbonate of soda, mixed spice and salt.

In another bowl, beat the eggs and add the sugar and carrot pulp to them, then beat the two sets of ingredients together. When everything is blended well, bake for around 25 min. in a greased cake tin until springy to the touch.

LOW GI CANNED CARROT LOAF

160g well-mashed tinned carrots
2 eggs
100g margarine
140g sugar
100g flour
half a teaspoon of bicarbonate of soda
a teaspoon of cinnamon or nutmeg
90g of currants or other dried fruit, chopped into small pieces if necessary
1 large or 2 small grated apples, including skin
2 slices of wholemeal bread, made into breadcrumbs with a food processor or grater

Pre-heat the oven to gas 4, 180C/350F.
Cream together the margarine and sugar.
Add the beaten eggs, then beat in the flour, bicarbonate of soda and spice.
In a separate bowl mix the currants, carrot puree, grated apple and breadcrumbs together then add to the other ingredients.

Pour the mixture into a greased loaf tin and bake until a skewer comes out clean from the centre: around 55 minutes. A lovely moist fruity cake.

Day 59: Sunday 30th September

There was plenty to keep us busy out of doors all day, walking the beaches and roads with our binoculars at the ready in search of bird life. We enjoyed the wild beauty of Barra despite the heavy showers. We popped home for a quick lunch before heading out to Vatersay, since there was an event I wanted to go to: a talk and film after a memorial service to mark the 165-year anniversary of the shipwreck of the 'Annie Jane' emigrant vessel on the west beach there. I'd read an excellent book on the subject and the author was attending; the community hall was packed with locals and visitors alike.

It was a quick and easy lunch as our tin today was a superfood soup.

DOUBLED-UP SOUP

One can of soup (mine was broccoli, pea and pesto)
One thick slice of bread with the crusts removed
A splash of oil
A tablespoon of cornflour
A teaspoon of vegetable stock/yeast extract/pesto (I rinsed out a pesto jar)
3-4 tablespoons of natural yogurt/crème fraiche/soured cream/double or single cream
1 tbsp chopped fresh herbs, e.g. chives or parsley

Heat the oil in a frying pan and add the bread, cut into 1cm squares.
Stir-fry gently until crispy and brown then take the pan off the heat.

In a saucepan, mix a little cold water into the cornflour. Gradually add a cupful more water.

Mix the stock, yeast extract or other flavouring into half a cupful of water and add that into the cornflour mixture, then put on a medium heat on the stove. Stir as the mixture thickens.

Once the liquid is bubbling, add the can of soup, rinsing the can with a little water.

Heat the soup but don't let it boil, then pour into two warmed bowls (you can warm them stacked together in the microwave with a little water in the upper bowl).

Sprinkle the croutons around the edges of the bowls, swirl your yogurt or other creamy garnish into the centre, and top off with the chopped herbs.

Day 60: Monday 1st October

A coupon for a discounted can came my way today! The Co-op occasionally prints one out along with your receipt, and I was delighted to find I was to get 50p off any canned fruit. Perfect! I resolved to scan the aisles on my next visit, in case there was anything new.

The sycamore leaves were beginning to drift along the roadsides and the heather was taking on its autumn hues. I enjoyed my walk to the shops and back in spite of the rain. The wind in my face was invigorating and the air smelt of seaweed and storms to come. Our ferry had left at 4.15 in the morning to avoid the next weather front and was already on its way back, racing ahead of the equinoctial gale. I hoped there was sugar on board as the shop's shelves were emptied already. However, I'd all sorts of substitutes to hand: golden syrup or honey for drinks, jam or sweetened yogurt for baking. If you've ever read 'Nella Last's War' and marvelled at her ingenuity with what little she could acquire, suddenly one missing ingredient doesn't seem such a disaster.

We had a can of organic vegetable hotpot for dinner, which I imagined would be thick and hearty as the label assured me it was. Sadly, it was thin, wishy-washy and, according to Bruce, 'had no flavour'. I did my best to beef it up with a substantial topping, but we both wished it had been a different can, such as vegetable chilli or leek and potato soup. At least I hadn't spent ages slaving over a hot stove!

<u>CHEAT'S HOTPOT COBBLER</u>

1 can vegetable hotpot or similar thick soup or stew
125g flour
2 teaspoons baking powder
a pinch of salt
50g margarine
1 egg
50g grated cheese

Rub the margarine into the flour, baking powder and salt.

Add the beaten egg, then mix together until you have a stiff dough. Add a splash of water if needed to hold it together but try to keep it as dry as possible.

Roll out the dough to 1cm thick, then cut into rounds with a cookie cutter.

Put 4 rounds on a plate covered with a clean, dry folded tea-towel or kitchen roll.

Microwave on high for 2-3 mins until risen and cooked inside. Repeat with another plateful.

Pour the hotpot into a microwaveable serving dish, cover and heat for 3 min.

Arrange the cobbler rounds over the surface of the hotpot and sprinkle with cheese.

Microwave for another minute or until the cheese is melted. Serve immediately.

Day 61: Tuesday 2nd October

We were beginning to get up in the dark. 7.15 was just light enough to put out our recycling bins and fix up the washing-line for my second day's attempt at getting things dry. The wind was pretty strong but I folded the laundry and pegged it well so it wouldn't end up anywhere else. Bruce was out and about as soon as possible, looking out for birds and chatting with passers-by as another day began. White horses leapt across Brevig bay and gulls hung suspended in the updraught over the hill, hoping for some kind soul to throw their kitchen scraps outside. They love dustbin day: the vaguely rotten smell of unrecycled leftovers is manna to seabirds.

I'd just got back to the house when I got a phone call: a friend had found an Isabelline Shrike at the northernmost end of the island. My mobile signal, surprise surprise, was down again, so I was lucky to get the message. This was a rare and exciting find and a bird I'd never seen before. Bruce was already up there, so I grabbed my binoculars and set off on foot, hoping to thumb a lift for some of the ten-mile journey. Alas, the road was very quiet, but three miles later I saw our car speeding down the hill I was climbing as Bruce came to get me. Within minutes we were both gazing at this lovely little Asian bird. To our amazement, it flew towards us and sat on the barbed-wire fence just a few feet away. It seemed as curious about us as we were about it: perhaps it hadn't met many people on its journey over the eastern reaches of the European continent. As the species does, it had created a 'larder' in a nearby tree by impaling a bee it had caught on a branch to snack on later. In the meantime it scoffed fox moth caterpillars and generally made itself at home. At last we left it in peace and made our way hungrily back to the house.

After yesterday's disappointing dinner, I was delighted to have drawn a familiar can for the day. It was the ever-versatile baked bean (the can that I'd won last month at the coffee morning) which I made into this thankfully speedy hot dish.

CHEESILY-MADE BEAN BURGERS

half a tin of baked beans
a few chopped fresh or dry herbs
a beaten egg
black pepper
half a dozen slices' worth of breadcrumbs, white or brown
80g Edam cheese
flour for dusting
oil for frying

Mash the beans with a fork or stick blender.
Stir in enough breadcrumbs to make a firm dough.
Add the egg, pepper and herbs and more crumbs as necessary to hold the mix together.
Divide the cheese into 4 chunks and with floured hands wrap a quarter of the breadcrumb mix around each chunk, making a ball with cheese in the centre.
Heat the oil in a frying pan and press each burger down into the pan.
Fry until the burgers slide freely in the pan, then turn and fry the other side.

Serve immediately: the cheese inside should be warm and melty.

Day 62: Wednesday 3rd October

Bruce was very happy to polish off the other half of our can of beans with his breakfast before heading out this morning. He set off with a couple of biscuits and a boiled egg sandwich to trawl the island for migrant birds just as dawn began to break.

Together we checked people's gardens as we headed for Castlebay. A whistle from Bruce told me he'd seen something: there above us was a Wood Warbler, more commonly found in oak woodland than on our rocky island with trees few and far between. We watched its lively progress among the sycamore branches for a while, then I headed off to the shops while he continued on his birding quest.

It was interesting to see how some cans disappeared within days and others languished in my magic box for weeks. Today's can had been there since the very beginning, two months before, and all that time I'd been eyeing it with a recipe in mind based on George Mahood's 'man versus can' project.

In his very funny book 'Every Day is a Holiday', George did a series of challenges based on named days or months. One of these was National Canned Food Month in February, for which his wife was detailed to buy him 20 cans of food and remove the labels, after he found such a random can lurking in the back of their cupboard.

His twenty recipes included such highlights as home-made fudge and chimichurri (a tasty South American sauce) as well as many hitherto uninvented recipes, such as beans and sausages in blackened Yorkshire puddings. Mmm. He found those three weeks, dubbed 'Man vs. Can' a positive experience which encouraged him to be more creative and thoughtful in the kitchen, and when it was all over there was "a can shaped hole in [his] life".

He said he'd made some delicious fudge with evaporated milk, so I got the can out and got competitive with something more in the Scottish tradition.

TEN MINUTE TASTY TABLET

400g sugar
150 ml evaporated milk
30g margarine
a pinch of salt
5ml vanilla essence
Nuts, choc chips, grated chocolate, biscuit bits, mini marshmallows or dried fruit

Bring the first 4 ingredients to a rolling boil in a heavy-based pan for 5 min, stirring with a wooden spoon, during which time the mix will start to thicken.

Take off the heat and add the vanilla and anything else you're putting in, stirring well.

Pour into a greased Pyrex-type dish. Cool then refrigerate overnight, if you can wait that long, then cut into squares and scoff. If you can't wait, the warm mixture is divine spread on a thick slice of bread or some toast!

Day 63: Thursday 4th October

The probability of drawing another can of beans had increased when I bought a four-pack for £2 the other day and added it to my collection, allotting the cans to the letters on my list wherever there was a gap once a food had been used. I was just choosing what was available in the shop, what was on special offer, or simply what I hadn't bought recently. The 50p coupon for a tin of fruit had been put towards apricot halves, since there were no new tinned fruits in the shop and I'd used the first tin of apricots right at the beginning of my challenge. Christmas goodies were just starting to appear on the supermarket shelves and I was hopeful there might be something in a can: chestnut puree perhaps, or mincemeat? So far, there were just fancy tinned biscuit selections. Hallowe'en and Thanksgiving were still to come, so maybe a tin of pumpkin pie filling might grace the shelves? I lived in hope. Anyhow, you can't have too many beans. I had an idea for an easy way to use my can today that would keep us well fed these busy autumn days.

<u>BEANY BAGUETTE</u>

415g can baked beans, pureed with a stick blender
250g flour
a tablespoon of herbs, fresh or dried
a pinch of salt

Pre-heat the oven to gas 7, 220C/425F. Put the flour, salt and herbs in a bowl, mix in the bean puree and stir well. Depending on the brand of beans, you may need a bit more flour or a little water: the mix should be just moist enough to hold together when you knead it with your hands. Roll into a baguette shape and put into the top of the oven on a non-stick baking tray. Keep an eye on it as it bakes and test with a skewer or sharp knife after 20 mins: it should come out clean when baked through. It may take longer, according to the circumference of the shape you're baking. A delicious and filling loaf!

Day 64: Friday 5th October

The sun was out and the wind had dropped. We'd been out until dark the night before, birding with our comrades. Before it was light, we had breakfast (bean loaf and eggs) and grabbed sandwiches from the freezer for lunch.

By trial and error, followed by a bit of internet trawling, I've worked out what's okay to freeze in a sandwich and why: peanut butter, jam, honey and tinned fish all come out just fine. Pâté made with oil rather than cream defrosts well as oil is a more stable emulsion. Any hard cheese, or tinned and fresh meats, will be good as long as there's no salad added, since it goes limp and looks nasty. Instead, dress the butty with pesto, mustard, horseradish, ketchup or pickle such as Branston or piccalilli and choose salad cream over mayo if possible as mayo tends to separate. Having said that, a bit mixed into grated cheese or coleslaw doesn't create a big problem: coleslaw made with salad cream or mayo comes out of the freezer rather less crisp but fine to eat. Make sure to spread the bread right to the edge with butter or margarine to help avoid sogginess. Make each sandwich airtight: plastic bags are better than plastic boxes as you can squeeze most of the air out of a bag, and pack more of them into limited freezer space. All that Girl Scout planning is worthwhile when you're in a hurry in the morning!

Then at the crack of 7.30 we strode out into the dawn, making the most of a beautiful day. Just before leaving the house, I fished out today's Scrabble letter. It was a W, and the can was chickpeas. In light of the busy day to come, I mulled what to do with it in the back of my mind as we walked up Heaval with our binoculars. Dinner was already sorted: veggie sausages, gravy and mixed vegetables with spuds from our garden. There was still cake or fudge to follow it if needed, but since it was the weekend, why not open the beer and have the kind of nibbles I used to enjoy in Spain as tapas?

SPANISH FRIED GARBANZOS

Crush a clove of **garlic** and fry gently in a good splash of **oil**. Add about 200g of well-drained tinned **chickpeas** to the pan (reserve the liquid for other recipes) and continue to stir-fry for around 5 mins. Sprinkle with a generous amount of **paprika**. Tear a few **spinach** leaves into small pieces and stir-fry for the last couple of minutes. Serve hot with beer.

Day 65: Saturday 6th October

It's crunch time: Walkers Crisps have caved in after the Britain-wide packaging protest and agreed to set up recycling facilities for their crisp packets by the end of the year! As I litter-picked my way once more around the football pitch, I daydreamed of a harassed executive at his enormous desk in Leicester, pulling his hair out as a lowlier employee delivers another three envelopes of empty wrappers to his brimming in-tray. "But these are from the Isle of Barra." he says, exasperated. "Is that even *in* the UK?"

"Yes, sir. Remote island in the Outer Hebrides," replies the post-room clerk, touching his forelock and beating a hasty retreat, all too used to his boss's temper. As he closes the office door, he hears a howl of frustration within.

"This is the last straw! We're recycling from now on!" the boss screams. Outside, his downtrodden underlings beam and high-five each other while he gnaws the carpet and foams at the mouth.

Well, I can but daydream. But it's certainly a result.

Today's tin is cherries-and-berries pie filling, so I delightedly fished my chilled chickpea water, saved from the previous day, out of the fridge and tried making a new dessert to celebrate.

I can't let the chance to tell my favourite joke pass by here: A man walks into a cake shop in Glasgow. "That cake in the window, is it an éclair or a meringue?"

The baker replies, "No, you're quite right, it's an éclair."

WHISKING GALORE CHICKPEA PAVLOVA

125 ml aquafaba (chickpea water) from a 400g can of chickpeas which has been refrigerated overnight

150g sugar

1 tsp lemon juice, cream of tartar, cider vinegar or white vinegar (it works without any of these but adding a little acid helps the pavlova to form and hold its foaminess)

a can of pie filling (mine was cherries, blueberries and raspberries with a hint of vanilla)

Pre-heat the oven on gas 1, 140C/275F.

Place a sheet of non-stick foil, non-stick side up, on a large baking tray.

Make sure everything you're using in this recipe is non-greasy. The tiniest hint of grease will flatten the whisked foam! In a very clean cold bowl, whisk the chickpea water with the lemon juice or other acidic addition until it forms peaks. (I did this laboriously by hand, using two forks held in one hand like a hand-whisk, but it takes a lot less time and effort if you've got a balloon whisk or an electric whisk.)

Whisk the sugar into the meringue, a very little at a time. The mixture should be airy and glossy, holding its shape.

Dollop the mixture onto the foil with a spoon, separating the dollops as far as possible.

Bake in the middle of the oven for 40 mins without opening the door.

Turn off the oven, still keeping the oven door closed, and wait a further half hour.

Open the oven, leaving the meringue inside and the door just ajar, for 30 more minutes, to cool.

Arrange the meringues in a circle around the edge of a pretty serving bowl, with the pie filling in the centre and more meringues on top, and wait for the amazement on people's faces when you tell them it's a vegan recipe!

Day 66: Sunday 7th October

The wind was wild and the rain lashing down, no ferries running and no planes either. We drove around just to avoid cabin fever, but every time we stepped from the car, hanging onto the door to stop it getting damaged, we were soaked in seconds. We couldn't see through our binoculars anyway as they steamed up straightaway, so we looked out to sea accompanied by the dreary percussion of the windscreen wipers, then gave up and came home. Chopped tomatoes were the can of the day, and since we had plenty of time thanks to the awful weather I invented a recipe to cheer us up and warm the room while it baked. I did the whole cake in one tin, but I was saving up some of my smaller cans, such as pâté and pineapple tins, to bake individual loaves or cakes someday. They'd bake faster, saving on energy as well as washing-up, and could be given as cute little gifts.

SWEET VEG CAKE

50g grated carrot

100g well-drained canned tomatoes, mashed to a pulp

80g dried fruit, chopped if in large pieces

2 eggs, beaten

60g margarine

half a teaspoon of bicarbonate of soda

140g sugar

100g flour

a couple of slices of bread or stale cake, grated into breadcrumbs

a teaspoon of mixed spice

Pre-heat the oven to gas 5, 190C/375F.

Mix the dried fruit into the tomato pulp with the carrot and spice in a small dish.

In a mixing bowl, cream the sugar into the margarine.

Add the eggs then the vegetable mixture, and finally stir in the flour and bicarbonate of soda, bit by bit. The aim is to produce a thick batter: add crumbs as necessary to reach dropping consistency.

Pour into a small greased loaf tin and bake in the middle of the oven, testing after 25 min. and leaving for longer if necessary. Cool 5 min. in the tin then tip out onto a rack. Slice when cooled and serve buttered at teatime.

Day 67: Monday 8th October

Everyone's mobile phone signal has been largely absent for a week now. Not so bad for those of us on Pay as you Go, but highly annoying if you've got a contract and can't get any use from it! Furthermore, being uncontactable makes us anxious that we may be missing information about migrant birds from our birding friends. Just like the old days, we tell each other where we're going and for how long, and pause on the road if we see another birder's car, just to check on one other's progress. So far we haven't missed out on any important news, and as for getting a lift home, someone is sure to stop on the road if they see me walking. I made a quick trip to the shop before I set off back for lunch, finding something new in the chilled section of the store, reduced to 50p. The can I'd drawn for the day was kidney beans in chilli sauce. Instead of adding lentils and veg. to our dinner, then, I stirred in this new combination of ready-mixed 'greens and grains': wheat, lentils, broccoli, kale, quinoa and edamame beans in seasoning. It meant the whole satisfying meal took just ten minutes to prepare. Linda McCartney had a 'Chilli Non Carne' recipe in the 'Home Cooking' book I mentioned earlier. It featured tinned toms and kidney beans, but it also had crumbled vegeburgers (what a waste!) or TVP, taking 45 minutes to put together. I'm sure it would be great, but I'm a bit too impatient to find out…

CHILLI NON CARNE PASTA

Cook enough **spaghetti** for two according to the pack instructions. Meanwhile, mix **a can of red kidney beans**

in chilli sauce in a saucepan with **150g of 'greens and grains' OR 100g cooked red lentils, a stock cube and 50g leftover vegetables,** finely chopped. Add **half a can of drained chopped tomatoes** and heat but don't boil. Serve the spaghetti in two large bowls with the chilli non carne generously poured into the middle of each.

Day 68: Tuesday 9th October

My wristwatch stopped last night. Years of teaching have made me dependent on it but it was still surprising how often I glanced at my empty wrist. I used it almost subconsciously when preparing food for later at the same time as breakfast, boiling eggs, making sandwiches and cooking the pink fir apple potatoes Bruce had dug up for our dinner. In exasperation I brought our alarm clock into the kitchen and resolved to mail-order a battery or a new watch.

The can was Napolina barley, a new product I'd begged a friend to bring over from the mainland. It wasn't clear from the description, ingredients list or the picture on the can if it was hulled or pearl barley, but I was pleased on opening it to reveal that it was the pearl variety. We can get the dry grains here but they take an off-puttingly long time to cook, so I end up doing loads all at once and then getting tired of it. This can-sized portion was just right.

MUSHROOM BARLEY SOUP IN MINUTES

Generously serves 2. Roughly chop an **onion** and fry in a good splash of **oil** in a large frying pan or wok until transparent. Meanwhile, crush a **garlic clove**, slice 200g of **mushrooms** and grate a **carrot**. Add the mushrooms to the pan, stir-frying until they're looking done, then the garlic, then the grated carrot, frying everything gently. Open your **can of barley**, and once the vegetables are looking ready, add the can with its liquid to the pan. Mix 2 teaspoons of stock powder or a **stock cube** into a canful of warm water and stir everything well. Bring the temperature up until the soup is bubbling. Serve with thick-sliced bread.

Day 69: Wednesday 10th October

I'd bought a can of black treacle when it was on special offer for a pound, and now at last the can came up. It would soon be Hallowe'en and bonfire night, and from my childhood I remembered the hard, chewy chunks of toffee my friend's mother used to make us for the exciting evening events. She shooed her many kids out of the way as she prepared it for fear they got burned: the stuff she stirred on the stove was like a cauldron of boiling oil and probably just as destructive. Even if it wasn't to our adult taste, I reasoned, we could give it away to trick-or-treaters (they call them guisers up here). Scots call this sweetie Claggum, which neatly sums up its texture.

WITCH'S EARWAX HALLOWE'EN CLAGGUM

2 parts **sugar** (e.g.200g) to 1 part **black treacle** (100g) and 1 part **margarine** (100g)

On a medium heat, stir all the ingredients with a wooden spoon in a large heavy-bottomed pan until the sugar dissolves. Bring up to a rolling boil and keep stirring. Have a dish of cold water at your elbow and from time to time test a teaspoonful of the mixture by dropping it into the water. The toffee should be firm but not brittle. I gave it around 5 minutes, so it was still a bit soft and chewy. When it reaches that stage, pour into a greased tray (a recycled aluminium foil oven dish – without any holes in the bottom – is ideal for this as you can flex it to get the contents out later) and leave to cool and set. Don't be tempted to dip your finger in it to taste: it's burning hot for a long time! When cool, break it into pieces. If it's very hard, take it out of the dish, cover with a clean tea-towel on a chopping board and break it up with a rolling-pin to enjoy a blast from the past.

There's another recipe I know of using black treacle, though it's not to everyone's taste. This, according to my friend Ruth near Falmouth, used to be what Cornish fishermen had to keep the cold out. It'll probably make you shiver when you knock it back, though not from the cold!

MAHOGANY

Mix 1 part warmed **black treacle** with two parts Plymouth **Gin**. Brace yourself, then drink it down in one.

Day 70: Thursday 11th October

I'd been reading my latest library book, 'Cooking with Tinned Fish' by Bart van Olphen, after hearing about it in a radio interview. It had some lovely pictures and a bit of interesting history about the canning industry, but of course the recipes were all about fish, in particular Portuguese sardines. Reviews were mixed: one simply said, "too much tuna!" but I sympathised with him on that: there are only so many cans to choose from after all. You can guarantee the fish will be as fresh as the day it was caught, though: all ready to cook with as soon as you open that tin.

I had a can of mushroom soup to use today, which I mixed with some leftover Mushroom Barley Soup and a few cooked new potatoes, chopped into chunks, to make it heartier. I heated everything in a covered serving bowl in the microwave while I made the 'lid' for our dinner:

RÖSTI TOPPING FOR SOUP OR STEW

Grate 200g of **parsnips or carrots**, or a mix of the two. Add 150g **grated potato**. Put the vegetables into a clean tea-towel and wring out to remove excess moisture. In a mixing bowl, sprinkle a tablespoon of **flour** onto the wrung-out vegetables, add a beaten **egg** and **salt and pepper**, and stir well. Heat a good splash of **oil** in a frying pan, then press the rösti into the pan with the back of a spoon, a maximum of 1cm thick. Cook for around 5 min until it smells done. Carefully put a heatproof plate over the pan to cover the rösti then turn it out onto the plate. Slide it back into the pan to cook on the other side. Once it's done, slide it carefully out of the pan onto the top of your serving dish of hot soup or stew and bring to the table immediately.

Day 71: Friday 12th October

There were gales howling around the island all night, but we slept snug and safe in our little house. Many locals had gone away to the mainland: it was half-term (a two-week break in Scotland) and now the height of the tourist season was over the pressure was off for many of the local workers. They were ready for a break. Armed with a pocketful of people's keys, I checked their houses and gardens the next day. The trip switches needed re-setting in one place and a fence was loosened by the winds in another, so I tied it up, but otherwise all was well. It was a struggle to be out against the weather, so I was glad to be back in the kitchen with my latest can. It was refried beans, evoking fond memories of my Mexican adventures. It had to be time for some lovely pastries!

<u>CAN EMPANADAS</u>

Take 225g **flour** and mix with half a teaspoon of **turmeric**, half a teaspoon of **paprika** and a pinch of **salt**. Rub 110g **margarine** into the dry ingredients to make a crumb-like consistency. Beat an **egg** and add most - but not all - of it into the bowl, reserving the last bit of egg in the fridge. Knead the mix into a dough adding a little water as necessary to get it to come together. Chill the dough in the fridge for at least half an hour. When ready to cook, pre-heat the oven to gas 4, 180C/350F. Flour your work surface and roll the dough half a centimetre thick then cut out circles with the rim of a mug or similar sized template. You should get 8 discs. Spoon a generous pile of filling (in my case, tinned **refried beans**) into the centre of 4 of the discs and top with another, crimping the edges together firmly with a fork to make the pies look full and plump. Make a few fork holes in the top of the pastry. Add a little water to the reserved egg and brush it over the top of the empanadas with a pastry brush, or use the back of a teaspoon to spread it over. Bake till golden brown.

Day 72: Saturday 13th October

It was wet and rainy. I had bananas to use up before they went too brown, and the can was tomatoes, also quite sweet, so I warmed the kitchen with an unusual creation at teatime. 'The Frugal Cook' by Fiona Beckett has a host of ideas to use up a bunch of bananas on their way out, from Chiffon Cake to honey mash with cream or smoothies with strawberries, blueberries and yogurt. She's ruthless about portion control and leftovers too: I imagine her whisking the dishes back to the kitchen as soon as everyone's served! She has some great-sounding recipes featuring everyday cans; one that caught my eye was her Two Vegetable Minestrone using a can of tomatoes and flexible additional veg. I'll give that a try someday. My own recipe went like this:

SMASHIN' MASH-UP TRAYBAKE

Pre-heat the oven: gas 4, 350F/180C. Cream 140g **sugar** with 60g **margarine** then add a beaten **egg**. Mash 2 medium **bananas** and 100g of drained **tinned tomatoes** to a pulp with a potato masher or stick blender and stir into the mix. In a separate mixing bowl, mix 100g **flour** with a teaspoon of **mixed spice** and a teaspoon of **bicarbonate of soda**. Add the wet ingredients to the flour mixture to make a batter. Pour into a well-greased baking dish wide enough to allow the mix to be 2-3 cm deep. Bake at the top of the oven, checking after 20 min and continuing to keep an eye on the bake until it's done. Leave in the dish to cool then cut through the mixture into slices. Serve with a cuppa.

Day 73: Sunday 14th October

Almost thirty years ago, when I went hitch-hiking through Africa, I found people in the south eating a delicious hot street food, served from someone's doorway and varying greatly in content though not in style. They hollowed out half a large white loaf and poured curry or stew into the hollow. Somehow the contents didn't leak through and every last bit was tidily eaten on the hoof. When I drew a can of vegetable chilli today, it seemed like a good opportunity to make a sit-down version that even recycles the can. The name is thought to be a corruption of "bhania", an Indian merchant, plus the slang word for food or a meal. The result is the African equivalent of the Cornish pasty.

BUNNY CHOW CAN-STYLE

A generous meal for 4 people. Pre-heat the oven: gas 4, 350F/180C. Find a baking tray large enough to hold a heatproof dish containing two canfuls of **curry**, stew, ratatouille or whatever you plan to eat with the bread, plus 4 upright cans. Make sure the oven has enough space for this tray to fit on a high shelf with room for the mini-loaves to rise inside their cans. Choose ring-pull style cans as they have a less hazardous sharp edge – but watch yourself anyway! Wash, dry and grease the cans with **margarine** using a pastry brush or a spoon with greased kitchen towel wrapped around it. In a mixing bowl mix 600g **flour** with a teaspoon each of **bicarbonate of soda** and **salt**. Add in a 500g pot of **full-fat natural yogurt** and stir to combine, adding a little water if needed to bind everything into a dough. Quickly bring the mix together with floured hands and divide into four balls. Push a ball carefully into each can and stand them on the tray alongside the dish of filling. Put the tray onto the top shelf of the oven. After 20 minutes start checking your little loaves and put out a cooling rack for them. Once they're risen and browned, turn off the heat and take the cans off the tray, leaving the dish of filling in the warm oven. Using oven gloves, slip a dinner knife around the inside of each can to release the loaves then ease each one out with the knife, leaving it to steam for 5 minutes on its side on the cooling rack. Put each loaf into a soup bowl, cut it two-thirds through lengthwise and take out some of the middle of the bread. Pour the filling into and over the bread and arrange the removed bread around the edge of the bowl. Substantial stuff!

Day 74: Monday 15th October

I went litter-picking with Bruce on Vatersay: after the recent storms there was quite a lot of plastic to pick up on the shoreline, plus the usual littering along the roadside. Beer cans, chocolate wrappers, and an empty champagne bottle lined our route; these people were clearly far too rich and important to take their recycling home. Why was no lackey on hand to do it for them? Anyhow, in the absence of any minions, I recycled their waste down at the supermarket into the big recycling skips. The carrier bag I'd used for the litter-picking was still a bit sandy, so I smugly mentioned as I packed my purchases into it at the till that I'd been litter-picking and the bag was being re-used. Five seconds later, as I bore it towards the door, the bag broke and Bruce's bottle of beer smashed all over the floor. The travelling distance of the sticky, sudsy foam, shards of glass and a pint of liquid was quite astonishing, not to mention embarrassing. The gunshot noise brought everyone momentarily to a standstill, then they all pitched in to help. I was even given a nice new bag before I slunk out of the door, having created a bit more recycling and a lot more work for the lovely staff. Well done Kath, I thought: that so served me right for being overly pleased with myself.

A birding friend's birthday was coming up. Can of the day was cider. It seemed like the thing to do was to make a cake to kill two birds with one stone. I hasten to add that no birds were harmed during the making or consuming of this cake!

<u>CIDER APPLE CAN LOAF</u>

Pre-heat the oven: gas 4, 350F/180C. Take a 500g pack of Wright's **ginger cake mix**, add 260ml of any variety of **canned cider** and 150g of **grated apple**, including the peel. Stir into a batter and pour into a greased loaf tin. Bake at the top of the oven for around 40 min while drinking the rest of the cider; have a look at it after half an hour and test with a knife to see if it's done in the middle. Spread with frosting and candles if you're feeling celebratory!

Day 75: Tuesday 16th October

I had a coupon for a thin-crust pizza so I got Bruce that for his dinner along with his favourite home-made coleslaw which coincidentally provides a home for at least one of your five-a-day plus many a leftover! Since the oven was on and I had some yogurt to use up, I also made an easy-peasy loaf using our can of the day: sweetcorn. The weather was rotten, which is probably why I chose another African-inspired recipe with bright yellow nuggets of sweetcorn nestling in the warm crust. Corn kernels are called mealies in Africa. I was glad I had a can that would create some speedy comfort food, studded with sunshine.

SLAW UNTO ITSELF

Grate half a **carrot**, some **apple**, and the least woody part of a peeled **broccoli stalk** or **cauliflower stem**. Add a tablespoon of drained **sweetcorn** and a heaped tablespoon of **mayonnaise or vegan mayo** (See Day 7). Stir to combine and add a little **oil** if needed to bring everything together. A colourful and tasty addition to your 5 a day.

CANNED MEALIE BREAD

300g flour plus extra for handling the loaf
1 tsp bicarbonate of soda
1 tsp salt
250g full-fat natural yogurt
80g well drained tinned sweetcorn (about 3 heaped tablespoons)

Pre-heat the oven: gas 4, 350F/180C and grease a baking tray ready for the middle oven shelf. Mix the first 3 ingredients together then add in the last 2, working quickly. Bring the dough together with floured hands, adding a little water if needed to make it into a ball. Put the ball on the baking tray and cut a deep cross into the centre. Bake for around 30 mins till risen and browned, testing the centre for baked-ness with a knife or skewer. Best enjoyed while still warm with soup or generously buttered.

Day 76: Wednesday 17th October

I don't often indulge in hen-napping, but for the second day running I noticed one of my neighbour's chickens wandering nonchalantly in the road on a sharp bend, far away from the safety of the henhouse. Bruce and I jumped out and grabbed her; she sat quietly in a Co-op bag as I drove her home to rejoin her friends, but there was no big reunion: nobody had missed her. She just backed out of the bag and carried on pecking and scratching as before, but within the confines of the yard. They probably wouldn't believe her adventures if she told them!

Back at the house, I opened our latest can for lunch. It was sweet chilli and lime soup with yams: quite exotic and not available locally, it had come from The Mainland. Over yonder you can buy instant noodles for 20p too: a third of the price of the cheapest ones here. I had a pack of such noodles in my possession so I made twice the soup in half a minute.

CAN-NOODLING AT LUNCHTIME

Take a pack of **instant noodles** (Sainsbury's Chicken Flavour ones are vegan) and crush them into small pieces while the packet is still closed. Pour into a mug or bowl, removing the flavour sachet, and cover with **boiling water**. If the flavouring complements your soup, add it in, otherwise save it for another recipe and add a little powdered **stock** or a crumbled stock cube to the noodles instead. Cover the noodles and set aside. Meanwhile, heat your **tinned soup**, rinsing the can to get the last bit out.

Combine noodles and soup in the pan, make sure everything's piping hot then serve in two mugs or bowls.

Day 77: Thursday 18th October

I had Mexican beans in chilli sauce to use today. Have you seen the film 'Once Upon a Time in Mexico'? Johnny Depp's character famously says, "Are you a Mexi-can or a Mexi-can't?" Well, when it comes to putting together this easy and tasty dish, I'll quote Barack Obama: "...yes, we can!" For this recipe I could have bought 8 flour tortillas for £1.30 in our shop, but home-made ones are cheaper, fluffier and softer, albeit less perfectly circular. That's not a bad thing: you can see they've been lovingly made just minutes before.

MEXI-CAN ENCHILADAS

Take a can of **mixed beans in chilli sauce** and warm them in a pan. Mix in fresh or canned **chopped tomatoes**, **sweetcorn**, **peas** and/or any other leftover chopped **cooked vegetables** you have in the fridge. Grease a flameproof dish and pre-heat the grill. Using either bought or home-made **tortillas** (see recipe below) roll some of the vegetable filling into each one (less messy if you do this inside the dish) and wedge them up against each other so they stay rolled up. Pour some **tomato passata** over the rolls. Sprinkle liberally with **grated cheese** and some **chilli flakes** if you like. Grill till the cheese is bubbling and serve immediately.

FLOUR TORTILLAS

Take an empty, clean and dry can (or any similar-sized measure) and fill it with **flour**. Pour the flour into a mixing bowl and mix with 1 tsp **salt** and 1 tsp **baking powder**. Half fill the same can with **warm water** and add in 2 tbsp **cooking oil**. Pour the oily water into the flour bit by bit and mix until you have a dough. You may not need all the water. Leave the dough to rest for 15 minutes then break off a chunk and roll into a thin disc. Cook on a medium heat in a greased frying pan for around a minute on each side, then put on a warm plate under a tea-towel while you do the rest of the tortillas. Serve straightaway.

Day 78: Friday 19th October

I did a questionnaire circulated by the Citizen's Advice Bureau called "Food on the Table" which was designed to assess the difficulties some of us face in accessing enough nutritious food. It looked at where we shopped, how we got to the shops and what we bought when we got there. They also wanted to know whether we had trouble affording certain types of food, such as fresh fruit, and whether they were readily available. What it didn't ask was whether we shopped with certain items in mind or with a price limit in mind: my chilled food and fresh fruit and veg. purchases are almost entirely from the "reduced to clear" section of the shelving. So I take what I can get! My groceries, likewise, are often bought with a coupon or when a special offer comes up. I don't care if things are at the end of their shelf life: we deal with those straightaway, keeping the less perishable foods for later. I'd love to stock up to buffer us against all the pitfalls which occur here, and if I did, my stockpile of choice would consist of cans. They don't go off. They're unaffected by power cuts or extremes of temperature. Rodents and insects can't get into them. They stack away tidily. The food's already cooked. You know exactly what's in the tin: the nutritional information's all there on the label. Cans can provide a reasonably-priced, ever-ready addition to our five-a-day, all year round. In the short time I've been doing my challenge, we've had power outages, gales, ferry cancellations, a freezer breakdown in the supermarket and loss of mobile phone signal, all for lengthy periods. We're vulnerable on our island and it wouldn't take long for us to run out of food and fuel. Of course, we're a strong and resourceful community and we'd all muck in to find a solution, but cans are a great standby, without a big financial outlay, to get through a food-supply crisis. After all, it's not even winter yet! It's an insurance policy: if we fell ill or couldn't get around for some reason, that little stash would see me through.

I had a can of tomatoes today, 32p, as well as some red plums, 30p (reduced to clear) and a sweet pastry case, similarly reduced to 25p. Tomatoes are not the only fruit, but sweet enough to put into a dessert, I reckoned. I was making something I'd never tried before, but I was feeling lucky…

TIN TOM FRUIT TART

Spoon out half a can of **tomatoes** and strain them to remove excess liquid. If you don't like the seeds, they can be removed at the same time (see day 51) but I left mine in. Put the tomatoes into a saucepan, mash down with a potato masher then stir in a teaspoon of **cinnamon** and 3 heaped tablespoons of **sugar**. Bring to the boil then start to simmer. Peel 5 ripe or over-ripe **plums** by dropping into a dish of boiling water for a couple of minutes then fishing out – carefully – one by one and plunging into cold water. The skin will come off easily. Remove the stones and add peeled chunks of plum to the simmering tomatoes. After 15 mins, the fruit should be getting nice and jammy. In a cup, mix a tablespoon of **cornflour** with a little cold water then add it gradually to the pan, stirring all the time until thickened. Remove from the heat, stir in 4-5 tablespoons of **apple sauce** from a jar (or home-made apple puree) and leave the fruit to cool (quicker if you transfer it to a cold dish) then when ready to serve pour into a **sweet pastry case** and decorate with **mini meringues or squirty cream**. Invite guesses as to what's in it!

Day 79: Saturday 20th October

The sun was shining, so we made the most of a beautiful day by walking for miles and checking all the gardens we passed for migrant birds. A couple of birders had made the long journey to see the amazingly orange Northern Oriole that arrived last week via a gale from the USA. We don't get many 'twitchers' here (birders who come to see other people's finds, to add them to their list of sightings) as it's a long and expensive journey, but we enjoy meeting them when they do come. Everyone who had taken the risk of not seeing the bird or of getting marooned by ferry cancellations had so far gone away happy, having made a contribution to the out-of-season Barra tourist economy and added a tick to their British list.

I'd drawn chickpeas again: what a fab food! So much you can do with it: I'd hardly scratched the surface of the many wonderful possibilities for recipes. 'The Chickpea Cookbook' by Heather Thomas (Ebury Press, 2017) points out that tinned chickpeas are just as good, and so much quicker and easier to use, than dried ones in almost every one of her 50 recipes. So why do all that soaking and boiling when you could be out in the sunshine?

This is another easy recipe: the French call it Socca, the Italians Farinata. It's a pancake-style dish normally cooked in a hot oven on a large oily tray, like a Yorkshire pudding only flatter. The trouble is, it takes a lot of time and a lot of fuel that way, so I did mine on the stovetop. Please don't shoot me, you French and Italian gourmets….

PAN CAN FARINATA

Put a drained **can of chickpeas** into a flat-based receptacle. Add 3 tbsp **cornflour**, a teaspoon of **salt** and a tablespoon of **oil**. Blend using a hand blender, adding enough **water** to make a thick pancake batter. (You could use the chickpea water, but as it's so useful to make mayo or meringues I'd save and freeze it instead.) In a heavy-based frying pan, get some cooking oil really hot then add enough mix to cover the pan base. Fry then turn it over. It'll break up into chunks but that's fine: it's to be served like tortilla chips. When the first panful is done keep it on a hot plate while you do the rest. Serve immediately with a dip and drinks.

Day 80: Sunday 21st October

We got up in the dark as usual, Sunday or no Sunday. Apart from a few vicious showers, the day stayed bright and we battled a strong wind to walk all around Vatersay, the sandy isle joined to the south of us by a man-made crossing which today was lashed with sea-spray. Another birder turned up to see the oriole; he told us he'd managed to get the next day off work to get home again, so he had just one day and two nights on Barra. To his delight he saw the bird, then we gave him a lift part-way back to his accommodation and advised him to keep an eye on the ferry schedule. Sure enough, Murphy's Law applied itself and the boat for the morning was cancelled. At least he had a cast-iron excuse to spend longer on his Hebridean holiday: it turned out to be his twenty-first birthday too so I'm sure the boss didn't give him too hard a time.

Today's can was vegetarian chilli, which Bruce adores. I had a pack of puff pastry sitting in the fridge so it was a matter of five minutes to get this dish cobbled together and on the way while we showered, Skyped and entertained friends with cups of tea and slabs of cake. We even made some snacks with the pastry offcuts to have with a glass of wine later. I had a special trick up my sleeve to make it look like I'd spent time and trouble on the presentation!

LAZY LATTICE PIE

Pre-heat the oven to gas 6, 400F/200C.
Roll out **a pack of puff pastry** and use most of it to line a greased baking dish, preferably circular. Trim the edges. Fill the pastry with **a can of vegetarian chilli** or another

not-too-liquid sweet or savoury pie filling. Re-roll the remaining pastry and cut 10 long strips, about 1cm wide, from it. Place 2 strips across the middle of the pie in the form of a cross, then add the other strips next to the ones you've already placed, putting them on the pie one by one, clockwise from the centre out. You'll get the illusion of a fancy woven lattice without having to do anything complicated! Press down the edges, trim and bake, checking after 25 mins. Serve when golden brown.

<u>PASTRY NIBNOBS</u>

Gather up **pastry offcuts**, roll out and cut into 1cm strips. Hold the ends of each strip then twist from one end to make pastry spirals. Press the ends of the spirals onto a greased baking sheet to hold them in place then sprinkle with large crystals of **sea salt** and **cracked black pepper**. Slip into the oven beside whatever's cooking and don't forget about them: they puff up and brown quickly. Remove from the baking sheet when cool and serve them standing up in a glass or jug, with drinks.

Day 81: Monday 22nd October

When I drew a tin of sweet and sour sauce today it set me thinking about Asian food. I fancied something different, tasty and attractive from my can.

The Japanese call them Yakitori, the Koreans Bulgogi. They're skewered chunks of meat, often cooked by the diners themselves in a special kebab restaurant or prepared at their table by a flamboyant chef with deadly-looking chopping knives. I watched big family groups, out for a special treat, enjoying this type of cuisine in noisily packed restaurants wherever I went in Japan and South Korea. I hadn't got any kebab skewers, but why waste them anyway when you could use chopsticks? Unlike the blunt, square-ended sticks from China, both Korean and Japanese versions are thinner with a sharper point, thus more suitable for skewering things kebab-style. They're re-usable too and mean less washing-up!

SWEET AND SOUR CHOPSTICK KEBABS

Prepare a pan of steamed **long-grain rice** according to the pack instructions. Meanwhile, in a frying pan or wok, stir-fry colourful chunks of vegetable such as **peppers, courgettes, sweet potato, mushroom or mange tout**. Add chunks of **halloumi or vegetarian sausage** to the pan, and when everything is cooked, warm **a can of sweet and sour sauce** in a covered microwaveable container. Spread the rice out in a serving bowl. Spear the vegetables etc. onto 6-8 chopsticks, kebab style, to halfway up the sticks, and arrange on the rice so the vegetables are in the middle and the ends of the chopsticks overhang the bowl's edges. Pour over the sweet and sour sauce (you could make your own if you prefer: see day 56) and serve at once.

Day 82: Tuesday 23rd October

In Hong Kong in autumn I was often given moon cakes, made with sweet bean paste and a whole boiled duck egg slap-bang in the middle of the dense pastry-covered mass. To explain the origin of the Chinese Mid-Autumn Festival, when the moon is bright and the harvest in, there's a legend about a goddess who went to live on the moon to save her lover, so perhaps the egg represents the moon. It's a very filling delicacy as you may imagine, so to celebrate our own beautiful full moon I chose to make something a little more familiar and not quite so heavy, though this is still a moist dense cake. Not having any sweet bean paste, I experimented with borlotti beans. These were the favourites of my old friend Paul Carter, who loved Venice, Grappa, and the novels of Marco Vichi. He entertained Bruce and I in Bristol on many an evening, and would have tasted my milky-brown hot chocolate-flavoured bean cake and said kind things about it!

BORLOTTI BEAN CAKE

400g can borlotti beans (or other drained and rinsed beans)
1 tsp vanilla essence
70g instant hot chocolate mix
1 tsp baking powder
1 tsp bicarbonate of soda
a pinch of salt
125g margarine
140g sugar
4 eggs

Pre-heat the oven to gas 6, 400F/200C.

Drain a can of borlotti beans and puree them with a stick blender. Beat in one of the eggs and the vanilla essence. In a mixing bowl, cream the margarine and sugar, then beat in the other eggs followed by the bean mixture. Add the dry ingredients and stir everything together well. Put the mix in a greased tin or dish and bake for 30 minutes then check the cake to see if a skewer or knife comes out clean: once it's done leave to cool in the baking container then turn out and cover in frosting if you like.

Day 83: Wednesday 24th October

There's been no boat since Sunday thanks to high winds and the shop is depleted of stock. That stranded young birder we saw has presumably gone up the island chain today via smaller ferry crossings which are less likely to be cancelled. It's a long, long way round: you get to the mainland north of where you expected to be, then hack back 86 miles down the other side to Oban.

The stranded-ness such a visitor may experience was underscored in a book I enjoyed from the '80s. 'A house by the shore' by Alison Johnson is the true story of a young couple setting up a hotel on Harris with almost no money. Their first cooker was rescued from where it had been dumped in a river, but once dried out it seemed to do the job. They couldn't get fresh food for much of the time, and detailed their struggles with sourcing ingredients and making do, not just for themselves, but for guests with high expectations! The small town of Stornoway was a full day-trip away, and the nearer village shops demanded a half-day excursion. Meanwhile, they had to clean, launder and attend to the rest of the housekeeping without any help. Fresh produce was available just twice a week, so she confessed to re-using leftovers and resorting to tinned French beans and tinned fruit in ice-cream while they tried to create a garden amid the chaos of their new business. In spite of their tribulations they got into the Good Food Guide, which assured their future success. Another happy ending for the Hebrides, and worth a read.

I was pleased to have some ingredients to hand in the cupboard to concoct my next can experiment: lychees. Bruce was particularly pleased when we opened the ginger wine and sat by the wood-burning stove with our nibbles and drinks.

STUFFED LYCHEES

Drain **a can of lychees** well. Sit them on kitchen paper or a clean tea-towel to dry. Meanwhile, open a pack of **cream cheese** and mix 125g of it with a dash of **ginger wine, rum or whisky** and a small handful (about 30g) of **sultanas**. If possible, leave the lychees and filling for around 15 min. at this point so that the lychees can dry and the dried fruit and cheese can soak up the alcohol's flavours. Then carefully stuff the lychees: it's a bit fiddly but best achieved with a small teaspoon and a bit of patience. Serve as a snack with a wee dram.

Day 84: Thursday 25th October

We had lunch out at the polytunnels' café once more to say goodbye to our birding friends due to leave in the morning. We had hot soup and a good chat before I gave them a couple of my latest baked slices for the road. Bruce said this recipe was the best of my efforts so far, with second place going to the chickpea pavlova and third to the lattice pie I did recently. Since my cakes were based on Mr. Kipling's almond slices, but contained no ground almonds at all, it was easy to give them a name.

EXCEEDINGLY GOOD FAKES

Make a small amount of shortcrust pastry (rub 1 part **margarine** into 2 parts **flour**, e.g. 100g marge with 200g flour, then add the minimum of **water** until you can bring it together as a dough) and roll it out. Line a greased square baking tin with the pastry. Spread any variety of non-lumpy **red jam** (mine was seedless raspberry) over the base of the pastry, around a third of a centimetre thick. Put the oven on: gas 4, 180C/350F. In a mixing bowl, melt 75g **margarine** (a few seconds in the microwave will do it) then beat in 100g **dry semolina**, 125g **sugar**, an **egg** and 2 tsp **almond essence**. Pour the mixture over the jam then sprinkle the top with a few **flaked almonds** or 3 or 4 whole almonds flaked with a peeler or sharp knife – carefully! Bake in the top of the oven for 30 mins until springy in the middle to the touch. Cool in the tin then cut into slices. A surprisingly almondy taste and texture!

I'd received another tinned fruit 50p-off coupon from the Co-op a while back and converted it into pineapple rings, and today my lucky can came up.

PINEAPPLE CHEESE PIE

Put about half a pack of any kind of **sweet biscuits** in a plastic bag (stale or broken ones are okay). Bash into crumbs with a rolling pin. Add a couple of spoonfuls of **sugar** and shake up together. Warm about 3 tbsp **margarine** in a small bowl in the microwave and mix the crumbs into it. They should be coated enough to hold together. If not, add more fat. Press firmly into the base of a glass flan dish and refrigerate. Open the can of **pineapple**, reserving a few pieces, and drain and finely chop the rest. Put a 200g tub of **soft cheese** (such as Philadelphia) in a bowl and add the chopped pineapple, a couple of tablespoons of **sugar** and 100g of **soured cream**. Stir to combine. Spread the mix over the crumb base and decorate with the remaining pineapple and anything else you fancy, e.g. glacé cherry halves or grated chocolate.

Refrigerate for about 4 hours if possible then slice and serve.

Day 85: Friday 26th October

It was grim drizzly weather again, so we had the washing hung around the wood-burning stove to dry because we'd run out of socks and reached Peak Pants: none left in the drawers! We sat companionably, Bruce on his laptop, me writing a shopping list on a recycled can label. Better to take these off rather than leave them to be burnt off the cans at the recycling plant; they're handy for 'notes to self' beside my keys before I hurry out of the door, or scribbled over with recipes using the product in the tin. The weight of the chief ingredient, plus its nutritional information, is right there on the back, and what I used that particular can for is documented in the obvious place. I've a sheaf of such recipes for future reference now.

On the subject of shopping, my friend Alice as a young mum got one of those tartan shopping trolleys, since she didn't have a car, and marched with her toddler and her pregnant belly to the Aldi a couple of miles away. She towed it back loaded up with cans much cheaper than they were sold at the parade of shops near to her house, and didn't worry a whit about looking uncool. Her family ate very well and she and little Emily got their daily walk, saving money at the same time.

While we sat in busy silence, our comfort food was simmering on top of the wood-burner. We shared a nice glass of cider from the can of the day while we waited, and felt a warm and cosy glow inside and outside.

BESIDE A CIDER STROGANOFF

a good splash of oil

1 onion, chopped, red or white
1 tsp paprika
1 tsp crushed black pepper
300g mushrooms, in chunky slices
2 garlic cloves, crushed
250ml sweet cider from a can
3 tbsp dry sage and onion stuffing mix (Paxo is vegan)
a pinch of dried thyme

Fry the onion gently in the oil, add the mushrooms and continue frying till they're browned, then add the garlic. Stir in all the other ingredients and simmer gently in an open pan for 20 minutes.

Take off the heat and leave the pan to stand for a few minutes with a lid on. Serve with rice or mashed potatoes.

Day 86: Saturday 27th October

We got a call from an islander not far from us, just as we were staggering in from another long walk over Vatersay. There was a strange bird outside her kitchen window; would we like to see it? With only an hour of daylight remaining, we hastened over to her lovely secluded garden with our binoculars, but sadly the bird had flown. Bruce writes a birding column for the weekly Barra newsletter, inviting people to get in touch if they see anything unusual, so we're used to that kind of call. And sometimes, just sometimes, we get a nice surprise.

Luckily, I'd already opened the can of custard I drew for today, and made it into a sacrilegious version of that revered Italian dessert we all know and love. We sampled it at our leisure after a hastily-prepared frozen pizza.

EASY TIN TIRAMISU

200g trifle sponges or leftover cake
150ml cooled strong coffee
120ml Tia Maria or any liqueur or spirit you have hanging around, e.g. advocaat, sherry or brandy
400g tin of custard
250g thick Greek-style yogurt
squirty cream or more thick yogurt
a dusting of cocoa powder or a little grated chocolate

In a trifle bowl spread out chunks of the sponge, then soak them in the coffee and liqueur. Mix the custard and yogurt together and spread it on top of the sponge and liquid. Leave the bowl in the fridge for a few hours if possible, then just before serving decorate with squirty cream or more yogurt and sprinkle with cocoa powder or grated chocolate.

Day 87: Sunday 28th October

Once again we spent the day walking over the machair, revelling in the late autumn sun. The clocks' changing had barely registered with us: we still went out at first light and ground slowly to a halt in the evening as darkness fell. I had a pretty uninspiring can of leek and potato soup to use today, so when we came in for lunch and to take the dry laundry off the washing-line, I whipped up a recipe that forced our can to stretch out for two hungry hikers. We like dumplings, but they need boiling liquid to cook, and tinned soup loses its flavour if boiled. Accordingly, I made micro-dumplings while the soup warmed gently on the stove.

MICRO-DUMPLING TINNED SOUP TEASE-OUT

Heat **a can of soup** on a medium heat, diluting it with half a canful of **hot water** from the kettle and adding a little stock powder. Don't allow it to boil. Meanwhile, half-fill a mug or small bowl with **flour** and stir in dried mixed **herbs**, **black pepper** or **grated cheese** to taste. (I put in all three.) Beat **an egg** and add 2 tbsp of egg to the flour with 2 tbsp of **oil** and 2 tbsp of **water**. Mix the flour into a dough, adding a little more water if necessary. (The rest of the beaten egg will keep in an airtight container in the fridge for two days, ready to add to another recipe or to brush pastry before baking.) Roll the dough into marble-sized balls, put half a dozen onto a microwaveable plate and cook on high for around 90 seconds until well puffed up. Repeat with the rest of the dough. Pour the heated soup into two bowls and float the dumplings on top. Serve immediately.

Day 88: Monday 29th October

I was judging the Hallowe'en Lantern Competition in the community shop, resplendent in a scarlet wig with a plate of Witch's Earwax Claggum (see day 69). I'd brought a couple of lanterns myself, one made from a jam jar wearing a ghost's shift of white tissue paper with a scary face, the other a recycled soup can with holes punched into it with an awl to create the outline of a ghoul with big glowing eyes. Bruce carried in a pair of more traditional carved pumpkins. Once we gained the shelter of the shop, we dropped tea-lights into each one and joined in the fun. There were amazing entries from all age-groups and the winners were very hard to decide on!

As for dinner: we like risotto. We like couscous. But I'd never tried making the Indian version of those. When a can of mushrooms came up, I decided it was time to have a go at this dish, which I'd watched people in India enjoying for breakfast. It seemed a bit spicy for that time of day to me, plus we like to get going in the mornings rather than slaving over a hot stove, so I made it for lunch with fewer spices than the original. National Curry Week was already over, but I could at least nod in the direction of luscious Indian food with this.

UPMA

Chop an **onion** and fry it gently in a good splash of **oil** until transparent. Add a can of drained **tinned peas** (or 150g frozen peas) and a drained **can of mushrooms**. Stir everything gently with a wooden spoon to heat it up then add a heaped teaspoon of **curry powder**, **chilli flakes** if liked, and 200g of **dry semolina**. Keep stirring to toast everything for a couple of minutes; meanwhile boil the kettle. Add **hot water**, little by little, gradually into the pan while stirring continuously as the water is absorbed. When you have a soft porridgey paste, give a final stir then put a lid on the pan and turn off the heat. Leave for 10 min. Serve in bowls with **coriander** or other fresh herbs sprinkled on the top. Nice straightaway but the flavours improve if you save some for the next day.

Day 89: Tuesday 30th October

This morning I was warming a few baked beans in the microwave for breakfast when it started making an alarming shorting noise followed by a series of lightning flashes from within. Mister Google told me that the waveguide cover was the name of the bit inside which now had a large hole burned in it. I did keep my elderly appliance clean, and dried it inside if I'd cooked something that made it steam up, but sooner or later all things must die I suppose. I'd got it from Freecycle in Shepton Mallet about seven years before, and the previous one was a Freecycle find too. We gave it a decent burial at the recycling centre, still commonly referred to as 'the tip' although the guys there do an amazing job of salvaging and re-homing anything from fridge shelves to firewood to anything else they get their hands on that still has some life in it. It's always worth asking them if they've a working version of the thing you're sorrowfully adding to their skips: we've been rewarded several times. This time we were unlucky, but there's always the Hebrides Freegle site (the new hippie love-child of Freecycle) or the Thrift, our very useful charity shop open once a week for just three hours. I resolved to check there at the weekend.

It's a good thing I'm fond of peas! I opened another can of Marrowfats at lunchtime and turned them swiftly into a filling lunch for one.

PEAS PLEASE ME SOUP

Pour a can of **peas** into a pan with their liquid and heat on the stove, adding half a can of **hot water**. Take a sachet of

instant soup (I used Tesco instant vegetable cup soup) and stir it in. Bring the pan just up to the boil then turn off the heat, still stirring. Season generously with salt and pepper or yeast extract. Pour the soup into a mug or bowl and enjoy with a hunk of **bread**.

Day 90: Wednesday 31st October

Hallowe'en is a big deal in the Hebrides! It's so nice that the kids can go from house to house in the dark with their friends, without needing an adult to protect them from perceived harm. We're told that 'stranger danger' is an outmoded message from the '70s and '80s which frightened children and demonised all strangers, while in fact most abductions are committed by someone the child already knows. It's a safer world up here in any case: more old-fashioned in a good way, with people looking out for each other and few happenings going unnoticed. We had seven 'guisers' this year: two adults and five very excited kids. They'd all gone to a lot of trouble to look scary; many of the kids had already spent a full day in face-paint and costume. We received a sparkly pumpkin, a satin-clad she-devil, a zombie schoolgirl, a skeleton, a robot, a beheaded child and a re-animated corpse. They told jokes, sang a song and shivered by the fire for a few minutes before blundering out (their masks making navigation tricky) to do it all again. We found the evening even jollier than Hogmanay as we didn't have to stay up all night: being up with the dawn every day isn't conducive to partying till the next dawn. And what if we missed a newly-arrived migrant bird by falling asleep? You snooze, you lose!

The visitors added some of my baking to their bags, including borlotti bean cake and prune cake from the freezer, plus a creation especially for this auspicious day.

CAN O' WORMS HALLOWE'EN CUPCAKES

Snap about a dozen strands of **spaghetti** in half and boil for around 9 min. Pour off most of the water, leaving just enough to cover the pasta. Add **red food colouring** and leave to soak in for 30 min. then pour off the excess liquid. Pre-heat the oven to gas 6, 400F/200C. Fill 6-8 muffin cases with **cake batter** using the fizzy-drink sponge recipe of your choice (e.g. Day 46 or Day 74). I did the recipe from Day 46 using **a can of Irn Bru**. Keep the empty can. Stand the cupcakes in the depressions in a bun tin. Bake on the oven's top shelf till firm and spongy to the touch: around 20 min. Leave to cool on a wire rack. An hour before serving, melt a bar of **dark cooking chocolate** either in a microwave or in a heatproof dish inside a pan of boiling water. Cover the top of each cupcake with chocolate using the back of a spoon. Embed a couple of lengths of red spaghetti onto the chocolate on each cupcake, tangled together like wriggling worms. While the chocolate is setting, put the can you used for the cupcakes in the middle of a serving plate. Put the ends of the remaining strands of spaghetti into the opening of the can, with the spaghetti hanging down around the sides like worms creeping out. Arrange the cupcakes around the can to serve.

Day 91: Thursday 1st November

I felt compelled to think about Christmas, if not to act upon it, now that the clocks had changed and the shop was filling with fancier fare. As we sat by the fire, I told Bruce of my ideas for decorations made from recycled aluminium cans, which I'd christened Foiled Again. Lanterns, like the ones I'd done for Hallowe'en, could be easily made with punched-out patterns such as snowflakes, bells or Christmas trees. If we went carol singing we could take them along, or leave them on the doorstep with a rock or some sand in the base of the can to stop it blowing away, and a candle on top of the weight. For a festive door-stopper, I planned to refill an empty can with sand or soil and put it upright in a Jiffy-bag, which we're sure to get plenty of when ordering books online. You tie up the opening so it'll stand up with a scrunched-together top, then drop the whole thing into the recycled wrapping from a Christmas present and gather with a ribbon or bow.

To Bruce's amusement, I leapt up and proceeded to construct a convection-powered table carousel using a small tin from pineapple rings with sand in it and a pencil, pointy-end up, stuck in the middle of the sand. I rooted around in the saucepan cupboard and produced a recycled individual aluminium pie dish, then pressed it like a hat onto the point of the pencil, right in the middle. The dish got a dent in it which allowed it to balance on the pencil. I then made little horses out of tinfoil and by means of a needle and thread hung them just below the rim of the pie dish. I lit a couple of tealights and nestled them in the tin on either side of the pencil. Once they were lit, the pie dish revolved slowly in the heat. This is a fun table centrepiece, but needless to say I wouldn't leave it or any other candles unattended in the house!

For our festive table, I might wash and de-label a couple of taller cans and put a bow around them made it from recycled wrapping paper if I'm feeling virtuous. I could put flowers or holly sprigs in them, or use them for Pastry Nibnobs (see Day 80). Then I could entertain my young niece with stilts made from food cans, re-purpose tins for baking as in my Bunny Chow recipe (see Day 73) or go outside to throw rocks at cans on a wall for target practice with her to let off steam if the cooking all gets too much.

It was National Sausage Week, which I'd never heard about until I heard some butcher on the radio talking about his sausages' closely-guarded secret ingredients. I had a pack of vegetarian Cumberland sausages stashed in the freezer from the day they were reduced to clear, so I brought those out to defrost and that evening made with my can of the day, chopped tomatoes, a nice tasty dinner in 15 minutes from start to finish. I'll divulge my not-so-secret recipe now.

STICKY SAUSAGE SPAGHETTI

Cook enough **spaghetti** for 2 according to the pack instructions. Meanwhile, roughly chop an **onion** and fry on a medium heat with a good splash of **oil**, stirring to prevent burning. Add 6 chilled **vegetarian sausages** to the pan and brown them. Open a can of **chopped tomatoes**, and if you wish, remove the majority of the pips plus any unappetising-looking bits of skin or core (see day 51). Once the onions are transparent and the sausages browned, pour in the tomatoes (wear an apron or tuck a tea-towel around yourself as the pan will spit) and add 4 tbsp **mango chutney** or any kind of non-seedy jam. Keep stirring well as the pan comes to the boil, then add **black pepper** and 1 tsp **paprika** if you like it. You may prefer to add dried basil or mixed herbs, or a tablespoon of red pesto; it's a matter of taste and of what you've got in the house! Let the pan simmer to reduce the liquid a little while you drain the spaghetti and divide it into two bowls. Warm the bowls with the drained pasta water if you like (see Tip, Day 25). Turn off the heat under the sausage mixture and divide each sausage into 3 chunks. This can be done with the edge of a wooden spatula while the sausages are still in the pan. Pour the mix over the spaghetti and serve piping hot.

Day 92: Friday 2nd November

I perused the supermarket shelves a little wistfully today: Heinz Big Soup was on special for a pound a can, but they only had two meaty varieties. We like the Chunky Vegetable one but it never turns up here; I even checked the convenience foods in "The Butcher's", not a butcher's nowadays but the home of our petrol pump, also selling newspapers, sweeties and snacks, but without success. When I read an Australian article later in the day about certain cans containing highly variable drained weights, then moved on to a UK Which? study on the same subject, I was surprised to see my coveted soup mentioned.

The team from Queen's University, Belfast, found that 23 of the 32 tins of Heinz Chunky Veg Big Soup tested weighed less than the permitted margin of error. So did an eighth of the cans of Del Monte Peach Slices, two being very underweight, plus 19 of the 31 Green Giant sweetcorn cans had less than they promised too! How irritating: I hate weighing things out when I don't have to. Just as well I'm not too particular about scientific quantities in my recipes, and not in danger of being underweight myself!

I had broccoli and stilton soup to use as my can of the day, so I added some of our lovely spuds from the garden, boiled but with the skin still on, to make it more of a Big Soup. Since we were microwave-less, it would take longer than usual to prepare it and wash up in any case, so I went the whole hog in my little Denby casserole dish in the oven.

CRUMBLE GRATIN TOPPING FOR SOUP OR STEW

Rub 50g **margarine** into 100g **flour** until the mixture resembles breadcrumbs. Stir around 30g **grated cheese** into the mix, and add **herbs, salt and pepper or chopped nuts** according to taste. Sprinkle over the top of your soup or stew and bake in a medium oven for around 20 min, until golden brown on top.

Day 93: Saturday 3rd November

A three-course meal from 2 cans of chickpeas? That's what Yotam Ottolenghi promises in the Guardian, using the chickpeas and "a few other store cupboard ingredients" to make "super-cheap recipes for students". I counted 37 ingredients in his meal idea: I had 14 of them in my cupboard, and could have bought or substituted about ten of the other 23, but it would have cost me an arm and a leg. The others just aren't available here. It looked like a lovely dinner in the pictures (soup, pancakes and ice-cream) but quite apart from the prohibitive cost it would take 45 mins to prepare the 3 courses then two and a half hours to cook them plus a whole night waiting for the ice-cream! I reckon most students would rather whip something up, write tomorrow's assignment while it's cooking, then scoff it with their mates straightaway.

The Student Room and other websites and books offer plenty of cooking advice for young people away from home for the first time. They advise lengthily on the 'essential' ingredients to bring with them to uni (this presumably is also aimed at the parents who are providing a taxi service for the youngster's mountains of stuff) as if there won't be a supermarket within a ten-mile radius. They need to learn to *shop!* This is a valuable life-skill: where, when and how, and how much to spend per trip. By all means start them off with some staples, and better still with stuff that's been lying around unused in the kitchen cupboard at home: they'll appreciate that nothing should be bought just to go to waste, and that making a meal from what you've got can be enjoyable and creative.

They'll have the internet: they can compare supermarket prices and grab the loss leaders. If they hunt instore for a cheap item they've seen online they'll realise that the store doesn't foreground generic brands or clearance lines: they'll be tucked away at the back of the shop or at the very top or bottom of the rows of shelves.

Looking in my own cupboards now, as a frugal shopper who buys luxuries from time to time but keeps the basics always stocked up, this is what I find, and this is all I'd recommend that even the most fretful parent provides for the teen leaving the nest (needless to say, the cheapest version available and just one pack of each):

Spaghetti
Penne pasta
Rice
Porridge oats
Packet soup
Granulated sugar
Eggs
SR flour
Margarine, 2kg tub for spreading or baking
Oil
Milk powder
Grated cheese (not tempting to grab a chunk to snack on and as cheap per kilo as a block)
Teabags
Coffee
Curry powder
Chilli powder
Cumin powder
Cinnamon

Mixed herbs
Black pepper in a grinder
Canned tomatoes
Canned kidney beans
Canned chickpeas
Canned peas
Canned baked beans
Canned butter beans

If there's a freezer, add a couple of loaves of the cheapest bread. That's about four carrier bags' worth and not many pounds' worth of groceries. They can read the labels, see the brand name and the store it came from, and carry on all by themselves. Learning's what being a student is all about, isn't it?

They'll learn about collaboration through cooking and shopping together or taking turns, and about when you're being taken for a mug by housemates who don't pull their weight or help themselves to your stuff when they come home late with the munchies. It's not a bad idea to stash a box of non-perishables under the bed in any case. It's all too easy to use more than you need if there's visibly a lot of something.

Leftovers, however, are a good way to make friends. And biscuits, scones, soda bread or pastries are cheap and quick to make and pass around while still warm!

I'd advise them to make up a week's worth of frozen sandwiches and just grab one in the morning, and to use a travel mug from home for coffees and teas, saving a fortune by doing so. They could make a habit of popping into the supermarket whenever passing by with five minutes to spare, especially late in the day, to get the reduced-to-clear bargains. These are valid life skills, whether they expect to fall into a well-paid job or become an unpaid intern after graduation.

Here's Yotam's list of storecupboard ingredients, which I doubt you'd find in the combined storecupboards of any hall of residence across the land. Take two cans of chickpeas of course, plus:

ground star anise
coconut flakes
flaked sea salt
strawberries
the juice of 4 limes
coconut cream
caster sugar
olive oil
salt and pepper
onion
carrot
celery
potato
thyme leaves
tomato paste
smoked paprika
garlic
vegetable stock
rainbow chard
red chilli
green chilli
flat leaf parsley
lemon
courgettes

chickpea flour
cornflour
coriander leaves
mint leaves
ground turmeric
ground cinnamon
ground cumin
fresh ginger
spring onions
cashews
vanilla paste

Blimey! Here's a link to the recipe if you're game to try it: https://www.theguardian.com/food/2018/oct/20/yotam-ottolenghi-student-recipes-three-course-meal

What would my equivalent 3-course meal be? It would serve two using just one can of chickpeas. How about a starter of home-made hummus and crudités, a main course like the one below, and a pavlova to finish (see Day 65)? The pavlova takes an hour and 10 mins in the oven then a half-hour to cool and dry, and has just 4 ingredients apart from the liquid from the chickpea can. The whisking part takes around 15 minutes or less with an electric whisk. My hummus takes 6 ingredients and 5 minutes. The main: 7 additional ingredients and 20 minutes. When I found my can today was apricots, I adapted another online newspaper's recipe to suit my own ends. Did you know that apricots are supposed to improve your vision and digestion as well as your skin tone? So says the Independent. There's certainly iron, calcium, vitamins and fibre in that sunny little fruit, whether it's dried, fresh or tinned. I read their tagine suggestion while deciding what to do with my apricot halves: they use dried fruit and more ingredients than you can shake a stick at. Having read it, I did a much simpler one instead, with good old-fashioned speedy couscous instead of trendy cauliflower rice.

TIN TAGINE

Chop two **onions** and fry in a good splash of **oil** until transparent. Crush a clove of **garlic** and add to the pan with 1 tsp ground **coriander**, 1 tsp **paprika** and **salt** and **black pepper** to taste. Drain and quarter the tin of **apricot halves**, reserving the liquid, and add the fruit to the pan with half a can of drained **chickpeas**. Add approximately 5 tbsp of **tomato ketchup** and 5 tbsp of **apricot juice** from the tin and bring everything up to a simmer. Pour in a little more of the apricot juice if the mix seems dry: you want the ingredients to be served in a small amount of sauce. Turn off the heat and put a lid on the pan. Make up enough **couscous** for 2 people according to the pack instructions and arrange in two bowls. Pour the tagine mix into the centre of the bowls and serve sprinkled with a little more **coriander** or chopped fresh herbs.

HALF-A-CAN HALF-A-MO HUMMUS

Put half a can of drained **chickpeas** into a blender cup. Add a tablespoon of **lemon juice**, a small-ish crushed **garlic clove**, half a teaspoon of **ground cumin**, 3 tbsp of **oil**, and **chilli or black pepper** to taste. Whiz to a puree with a stick blender, adding a little water if the result is too thick. Serve with carrot sticks or tortilla chips as a starter or snack with drinks.

Day 94: Sunday 4th November

I tried to heat a piece of ratatouille pie under the grill at lunchtime since I had no microwave: it had been in the freezer and de-frosting all morning, but the result was still cold and nasty in the middle. Bruce gamely ate the hot bit, but it was pretty off-putting. Never one to waste good food, I peeled off the pastry from what remained and threw it to the birds, who descended on it in seconds. The leftovers from the filling went into my soup pan, to be joined later by one of my Everyday Value sachets of soup and a mugful of water. It didn't taste bad at all.

Our laptop was on strike: it refused to do anything except sulk in the corner. Since it was blowing a gale and too rainy to enjoy a walk, we drove it to a savvy friend who gave it TLC followed by a stiff talking-to and a complete stripping down of its memory. Thank goodness for someone both knowledgeable and local! I'd been reduced to bashing away at our ancient laptop, which has no working number 2 or W keys. If you've ever seen the Stephen King film "Misery", you'll remember him being forced to write a book for a madwoman using an ancient typewriter. I felt a little like that. Never mind, this is the place to make do and mend, and we bore away a repaired laptop with great joy later. On to the next concern: what to do with a great big can of pink grapefruit? In chilly November weather a grapefruit and feta salad didn't sound very inviting. I decided to do something using those two complementary ingredients but with a more comforting result.

PINK GRAPEFRUIT CAN CANAPÉS

Pre-heat the oven to gas 6, 400F/200C. Roll out a sheet of **ready-made puff pastry**. Cut discs to fit a greased Yorkshire pudding/bun tin using a cookie cutter or the rim of a mug. Press each disc into a depression in the tin. Put a heaped teaspoonful of **cranberry sauce** into each, then add a couple of pieces of drained **tinned pink grapefruit**. Top with a generous amount of crumbled **feta cheese** and bake until the pastry is risen and browned: around 15-20 min. Serve hot or cold with drinks: the syrup from the tin is nice with a tot of gin over ice cubes!

If there's pastry left over, there's a sharing recipe I often make to use it up, baking it at the same time for just a few minutes.

TEAR-AND-SHARE DABBY-DOUGHS

Roll out your leftover **puff pastry** and cut roughly into 1cm-ish strips. Arrange them closely side-by-side on a sheet of foil or recycled aluminium dish/tray. Sprinkle liberally with **grated cheese, herbs, black pepper, chilli flakes** or anything similar you want to use up. Put in the top of the oven at whatever temperature it's already baking at (from moderate to high), allowing the strips to rise and meld into each other until they're browned and puffed up. This doesn't take long, making these snacks a good starter while the main dish is still on the way. Slide the pastry off onto a plate and let everyone help themselves to a piece as they sip their drinks.

Day 95: Monday 5th November

I'm still missing my microwave, having asked again at the recycling centre and the Thrift at the weekend. Ho hum. I'll haul the slow cooker out of the cupboard and get the oven going more often. It's expensive here though: we just received half a tank of LPG gas and it was almost £340. We'll make it last a long, long time.

While waiting for the delivery guy, I sorted out the last of our home-grown carrots. Bruce had already harvested the potato crop, which was safe in a sack for the weeks ahead. The parsnips were still in the ground, ready for Christmas. He'd washed the carrots and I went through them, peeling and cutting out imperfections. There was a bagful of scraps for the Eriskay ponies by the time I'd finished, and a container of prepared vegetables in the fridge waiting to be made into soup.

I had another failure in the evening. I was trying to make fudge using the can of the day, evaporated milk. Although I deviated only slightly from the can manufacturer's online recipe, it refused to set. Here's what I did:

BODGED BUDGET FUDGE

Put 200g **sugar** and 60g of **margarine** into a heavy-bottomed saucepan. Add 4 tsp of **instant hot chocolate** then pour in a 170g can of **evaporated milk**. Add 90ml of **water**, rinsing the can out with some of it to use every drop of the can's contents. Bring the mixture slowly to the boil, stirring continuously, then simmer while stirring for 15 min.

(At this point you're supposed to take the pan off the heat and whisk the thickening mix for 10 minutes as it cools. Mine didn't thicken, nor did the fudge made by numerous disgruntled commentators on the product's website!) To be fair, there were 50 reviews from happy fudge-makers, but it is supposed to be an easy recipe…

Anyhow, after a glass of wine and a few deep breaths, I allowed the mix to cool. Then I poured the golden syrup-consistency goo back into the pan and tried again, adding 100g more sugar.

BUDGET FUDGE TAKE TWO: YES WE CAN!

Ingredients: the same as previous recipe but *300g in total* of sugar. Be prepared to devote half an hour of your undivided attention to fudge-making, so pour yourself a glass of wine. Bring the ingredients *slowly* to the boil and stir continuously to prevent it from sticking or burning. Keep it at a *rolling boil* for *15 minutes* then remove from the heat and beat the fudge patiently for *10 minutes* as it thickens. Pour into a greased dish (a recycled aluminium baking tray works well as you can bend it away from the fudge once it's set). Put aside to cool. Finish your wine then put the cooled tray into the fridge to chill until you're ready to cut it into squares and sample it.

This time it was soft, smooth, dense and creamy, and properly set, without the graininess or brittleness of Scottish tablet. I'm assured, by the way, that a sugar thermometer is absolutely essential for novice confectioners. You decide! I managed without, using my usual seat-of-the-pants trial and error, dogged persistence and a stubborn refusal to waste anything. The first effort would have been spread on bread or poured over ice-cream if it hadn't succeeded second time around. If it had turned out with more bite, firm enough to snap into chunks instead of cutting, I'd have christened it Tin Can Tablet and considered it a result. If you've bothered to read this far, you've no doubt got the measure of my attitude to life in general and cooking in particular, so what you make of it is up to you!

Day 96: Tuesday 6th November

I was pottering along in Castlebay, noticing the ferry was still stuck in port with technical issues, when a van pulled up beside me. Was I still looking for a microwave, asked the driver. Yes I was! Well, if I went into the Thrift on Saturday I'd find a working one awaiting me. Fantastic! So works the Barra grapevine: people remember you and do their best to help. We all look out for each other, in every sense of the word. The coastguard, originally from Ireland, had stopped to give me a lift that morning, and he and I had remarked on how much like forty years ago Barra was – in a good way.

In the absence of a microwave, I'd brought out the slow cooker to make lunch. I had a fancy tin of passata with basil to use today, and it seemed a shame just to spread it over a pizza base. After breakfast, I got everything ready in the space of ten minutes and left it on 'low' to await our return.

PASSATA RICE SOUP

Peel and finely chop **two carrots** and **two onions**. Fry gently in plenty of **oil** until the onion is transparent. Meanwhile, boil a litre of **water** and open **a can of passata**. Pour the passata into the slow cooker and rinse the can out with a little of the water. Add enough **stock cubes** to the rest of the water to make a litre of stock. Pour into the slow cooker and add a tablespoon of **sugar** and two tablespoons of red or white **wine vinegar or leftover wine**. Weigh out 150g of uncooked **long-grain rice** and add it into the pot, followed by the fried carrots and onions and the oil they were fried in. Stir everything well then put on the lid and leave the slow cooker on low for at least 3 hrs. Enjoy a hearty and filling soup for lunch or dinner.

Day 97: Wednesday 7th November

Reduced to my last ten cans, I took out the Scrabble letters from A to J and randomly picked the four foods I'd be using over the final days of my challenge, writing the day of the week with a magic marker on the end of those final tins. I felt curiously sad to be almost finished, but when I told Bruce we'd almost reached a hundred days, he punched the air and said, "Yesss!"

We're both fond of the commercial brand of refried beans that costs around £1.50, but since they're made of pinto beans which are almost a pound cheaper, I decided to see whether I could make my own refried beans with today's can. There were a few remaining spinach and chard leaves in the garden since the gales whipped them mercilessly against the ground and brief, sharp hailstorms flailed the plants. I rescued them to make a green salad to go with our dinner.

MEAN REFRIED BEANS

Open and drain **a can of pinto beans**. Put a crushed **garlic clove** into a pan with a splash of **oil** and fry gently. Stir in the beans with a teaspoon of **cumin powder**, a teaspoon of **chilli powder**, a pinch of **salt** and a tablespoon of **wine vinegar or leftover wine**. Still on a low heat, stir everything for 5 min. until well heated. Take the pan off the heat and mash the mixture down with a fork or potato masher. Stir in **hot water**, little by little, until your beans are a mashed-potato consistency. Enjoy hot or cold.

Because I now had my home-made refried beans, a couple of avocados and the wherewithal to make tortillas, I thought I'd have a go at a vegan dish I enjoyed in the southern states of the USA as well as in Mexico. Burritos, so named because the folded wrap is supposed to look like a donkey's ear, ('little donkey' in Spanish), are a handy fast-food option on their own or a tasty dinner with some avocado slices and a bit of potato salad on the side.

BURRITOS

Cook enough **long-grain rice** for 2 according to the pack instructions. Meanwhile, mash an **avocado** with **salt and pepper** and heat some **refried beans**, either ready-made or made from the recipe above. Either make some **flour tortillas** (see day 77) or warm up store-bought ones in the microwave or oven. Stir 2 tbsp fresh or dried chopped **coriander** into the cooked rice and add **chilli powder or chilli sauce** (e.g. Tabasco) to taste. Put a tablespoon of the rice into the centre of one tortilla and add a tablespoon of refried beans. Add a little mashed avocado. Fold in the ends of the tortilla then the sides, so the filling is enclosed in a sausage-shaped parcel. Repeat, making a couple more per person, then serve with salad.

Day 98: Thursday 8th November

Earlier this week, I heard a radio discussion about stocking up on cans in case of shortages due to Brexit. A writer, Jane Fae, was spending an extra tenner a week on tinned pears, tomatoes, beans, evaporated milk, tuna, corned beef, Spam and cat food (for her pet, obviously!). This was on top of her £150-a-month normal grocery shop. She was concerned that insecurity about what next March will bring would prompt panic buying and consequent shortages in the shops. She's not alone: many people are buying up medicines or things not made in Britain, such as Marmite and olive oil. Fae predicted price hikes even if the foods she wanted were available, and since she didn't have a large shopping budget, she'd adopted a wartime mentality. Analysts call this "cocooning": storing up supplies in times of uncertainty. She stressed that for her it was a 'just-in-case' response, and that the food wouldn't be wasted: she'd be more self-sufficient if there was a spell of extreme weather, or she got ill, or somebody went on strike. It seemed, in view of the Spam and bully-beef, to be a very war-era British plan of action, and she admitted she was "channelling Granny" although stockpiling has been condemned as 'un-British' and 'alarmist'. Some predict the collapse of Sterling and the imposition of tariffs, plus the impeding of trucks bringing food to the UK because of unfamiliar new customs rules or even malicious delaying of drivers to punish us for leaving the EU.

I know a Dutch customs officer: she's had her Christmas leave cancelled due to extra work. The Netherlands is hiring another thousand customs officials to deal with the consequences of all of this; would it be surprising if some were a little peeved about all the changes?

Who knows if there will be hold-ups, and whether their purpose will be to humiliate Britain? I do know there aren't enough import licences to allow the changeover period to go smoothly, and that the snippets of information that leak out make people anxious. There are no longer warehouses behind supermarkets with several days' supply for the store. In 2000, the truckers' petrol strike meant that the shops were out of food within three days. The German Lidl and Aldi chains will deliver to the UK, deal or no deal, but will they still be as cheap? A spokesperson from the British Retail Consortium said they had not been approached by the government about all this, and that "our food supply chains are extremely fragile".

Even if you're not crazy about tinned food, it sounds to me like there's a case for having some in the house. This year, every Swedish household got a booklet from their government called "If Crisis or War Comes". It makes interesting reading, with pictures of people abandoning their homes, seeking refuge and packing up tins of food for the family. In a nation which still provides a nuclear bunker space for every citizen, they recommend storing 9 litres of water, enough for 3 days, and a supply of food. The great thing about tinned stuff is that, being already cooked, you don't need to add water, and it's often packed in drinkable liquid. With a shelf-life of several years, there's no harm in anyone, anywhere having a month's worth in the house, surely. Ian Jack, a veteran writer for the Guardian, wrote that in the '50s and '60s tinned food improved the eating experience of children scarred by wartime meals of gristly offcuts and stuff disguised as other stuff. He says "the tin…expanded our gastronomic horizon". You know what you're getting when you open a can. Predictability can be good if crisis or war comes…

Lord Woolton, British Minister of Food, had a pie invented in the last World War in his quest for a nutritious meal that didn't make a big dent in precious rationed items; it was named Woolton Pie in his honour. It didn't need any fancy cooking equipment to make it, or even electricity, if you had another fuel source for the oven. The original recipe called for fresh cauliflower, potatoes, carrots, parsnip, swede and spring onion, which may have been grown in your own garden or that of your friends or family. It also had grated raw potato in the pastry to save on precious butter or lard, which were rationed, creating a stodgy greyish crust which would certainly fill you up. The whole dish would weigh about 3kg: you'd need the muscles honed while working down at the munitions factory just to get it in and out of the oven!

Nowadays, margarine is cheap, and tinned goods frequently cheaper than fresh ones. If you fancy trying the pie, a sort of pastie in a big dish, you can throw it together a lot quicker than the original boiled, peeled and grated version if you use cans. Numerous takes on the original recipe are out there on the WorldWideWeb if you've got an afternoon to spare:

https://the1940sexperiment.com/2016/03/13/the-original-lord-woolton-pie-recipe-no-151/

To compare past and present food hardship, I've added up the prices of the items in the Co-op to calculate the total cost of my tinned-food pie at £2.95, compared with what the fresh items for the original recipe would cost in the same store: a bag of new potatoes on special offer, 79p, a cauliflower, £1, bag of carrots, 65p, a swede, 79p, spring onions, £1, bag of parsnips, 79p. Total including pastry: £5.22! Okay, you'd have loads of veg left over, and you might be able to source home-grown stuff, but still, you have to prepare and cook from scratch yourself which takes time and extra money, not to mention the money you don't earn in your munitions factory (or modern-day call centre) while you're making it. If there was no heating or electricity, my version of the pie minus the pastry could even be eaten cold at a pinch! Here's my contemporary take on the dish:

LORD WOOL - TIN PIE

Pie filling:
1 can broad beans including liquid from can, 59p
1 can baked beans, 32p
1 can sliced carrots, including liquid from can, 35p
2 cans of new potatoes, drained, £1.10
a medium onion, finely chopped, 17p
a stock cube, 20p
a tablespoon of rolled oats, 2p
Pastry: (about 20p for all ingredients)
200g flour
100g margarine
half a teaspoon of salt
a little water

Put the oven on: gas 6, 400F/200C.

Put the broad beans and carrots, with their can liquid, and the chopped onion into a saucepan with half the drained potatoes, cut into large chunks, plus the stock cube and oats. Stir then simmer for 5 min, meanwhile mashing the remaining potatoes. Remove the pan from the heat, stir in the mash and the baked beans with their sauce, and spread the mixture into a baking dish.

Add the salt to the flour, rub in the margarine then add just enough water to make a dough that sticks together. Roll out a piece large enough to cover the pie dish, cut to fit and make leaf or heart shapes with the remaining pastry to decorate the top of the pie. Cut a couple of slits in the dough to let out the steam.

Bake until the pastry is firm and brown (check after 20 min.). Serve with gravy and a tin of peas.

Woolton Pie was, to my mind, the wartime equivalent of Baked Bean Lasagne, which makes the most of ingredients cheaply and easily available to 21st-century people with limited time and money. Today's tin was baked beans; this is one way to make something different with them. I've highlighted the difference in prices between two supermarkets since to many people who don't have transport, this is the difference between having the money to make a dinner and having beans on toast again.

BAKED BEAN LASAGNE

a can of baked beans, 23p in Asda, 32p our shop
a pack of lasagne sheets, 45p in Asda, 56p our shop
a carton of tomato passata such as Asda's: 500g for 35p, 79p our shop

dried herbs such as Asda mixed herbs: 37p Asda, £1.75 our shop

instant vegetable cup soup, 25p for 4 sachets, Asda, £1 our shop

100g grated cheese, 50p, Asda, £1.10 our shop (from the smallest available packs)

Optional: a few leaves of baby spinach or rainbow chard, washed and de-stalked.

So the cheapest available ingredients cost in total £2.15 from Asda, with enough left-overs to make two servings of herby pasta soup another day. The same shopping in our local store costs £5.52. Not such a bargain, but the journey to Asda would cost a great deal from here! Although 'home delivery' (actually to a warehouse on the north side of the island) is possible to Barra, it incurs a charge of course, and you still have to go and fetch it or persuade someone to do so for you.

Put the oven on at gas 4, 350F/180C.

Boil a kettle containing around 500ml of water.

In a shallow heatproof dish, pour some of the boiling water over half a dozen lasagne sheets spread out individually.

Open a can of beans and pour a third of the can into the bottom of a small square ovenproof tin or dish. Add a good dash of passata and a pinch of herbs.

Using tongs or a pair of forks, fish out enough lasagne sheets to make a layer over the beans.

Empty 2 sachets of instant soup mix into a mug. Add enough boiling water to make an extra-thick soup. Pour half of this over the sheets.

Soften a few more lasagne sheets in the same way as before and put them over the soup layer, then add half of the remaining beans with more passata and herbs. Cover with more pasta and pour in the last of the beans with a decent amount of passata and herbs. If you're using spinach or chard, replace this last-but-one lasagne layer with the uncooked vegetable leaves laid out in the same way as the pasta.

Put on a final layer of lasagne sheets and cover with the rest of the soup. Sprinkle the grated cheese over the top and put the dish onto the top shelf of the oven for 20 min, then turn the oven off without opening the door. Ten minutes later, take out the lasagne and serve with salad or green vegetables.

Day 99: Friday 9th November

After the quintessentially British dishes I'd preoccupied myself with, I fancied something from more distant shores. Black beans were the can of the day, and I remembered having a dish that featured them wherever I went in Nicaragua. Gallo Pinto is made all over Central America, with dried beans soaked overnight then boiled, garnished with fresh coriander. It's tasty and filling, especially with some piquant sauce to liven it up. The name means 'speckled rooster' which is what it's supposed to look like. We had veggie sausages with it and ate it out of bowls by the fire with ginger wine to hand: just right for a dark night with a howling gale outside.

GALLO PINTO

Boil enough **rice** for 2 according to the pack instructions. Meanwhile, fry a small finely chopped **onion** in a large pan using a good splash of **oil**, then turn off the heat below the pan. Heat **a can of black beans** and drain them. When the rice is done, stir it into the onion in the frying pan and add the hot beans. Arrange in two bowls with fresh or dried **coriander** sprinkled on top and **spicy sauce** (such as Tabasco) added to taste. Top with fried vegetables or any other fried foods that team up well with rice.

Day 100: Saturday 10th November

The last day of my challenge had crept up on me: it didn't seem possible that tomorrow I wouldn't be fumbling in a bagful of Scrabble tiles or wielding a can opener – unless I wanted to! The final can, which had been sitting around for weeks on end, turned out to be cheese-filled ravioli. Well, I'd have to think of something different to do with those little pasta parcels. Since I'd made far too much rice the day before, I'd already decided on the starchy component of today's dinner. I remembered in Hong Kong my Filipina friend Rose explaining how to make her amazing special fried rice: her secret was really cold rice and a seriously smoking-hot frying pan. To top off that nostalgia-trip recipe, I invented something cheap, quick and cheerful.

RAVIOLI CHEESY SKEWERS

Heat **a can of cheese ravioli in tomato sauce**. Meanwhile, fry slices of **halloumi** in a little **oil**, making the pieces half a centimetre thick and about as wide as the ravioli parcels. Drain some whole pitted **black olives** and dig out 2 sets of chopsticks. Spear a piece of pasta with a chopstick, then a piece of ravioli, then an olive, and repeat. Use up all the ingredients like this on all 4 sticks then place the sticks on top of fried rice (see recipe below) with the sauce from the ravioli over them. Enjoy piping hot.

SPECIAL FRIED RICE

Heat a large frying pan or wok with a good dash of **oil** until it's very hot. Meanwhile, take your **chilled cooked rice** out of the fridge, beat **2 eggs** and crush **a clove of garlic**. Either drain **a large can of peas** or take 200g of uncooked frozen ones and put the ingredients ready by the pan so you can work quickly. Throw the garlic in the pan and stir for a few seconds, then add the cold rice. Keep stirring to get all the rice toasted and the oil mixed in. Once the rice is fried, add the peas and eggs to the pan, stirring the whole time. When everything's hot, heap into two rice bowls and top with ravioli skewers as above, another kind of kebab (see Day 81) or your favourite vegetables in sweet and sour sauce (see Day 56).

That was it: my challenge was over already! After dinner, glass of red in hand, I talked to Bruce and realised I'd learned a lot over the past hundred days. I'd done a lot more baking and improved or refreshed the skills my Home Economics teacher had attempted to din into me. As I'd hoped from the beginning, I've become slightly better at cooking, or at least more efficient at it! My imagination was given free rein and I played with ingredients to my heart's content.

One thing I'll carry away with me is that almost anything will make a soup, and my stick blender is my new best friend. Soda bread and its variations are going to feature more frequently on the menu from now on; I'll try using flavoured yogurts in breads and cakes too. This spirit of experimentation has helped me to become more inventive and knowledgeable about herbs, spices, their uses and their stand-ins. I've used ingredients we've never tried before, and substituted items on a recipe list for whatever I had or could get hold of here. My kitchen equipment has been given a good workout: I've done more with implements normally sitting idle in the cupboards and made do without things I couldn't get hold of.

I've re-visited memories and travel experiences and re-invented some of the dishes I had around the world.

I've thought, really thought, about where our food and its packaging comes from and goes to. This has made me become more committed to avoiding waste: I found cans are a good way to do that, and the learning process continues as I find ways to spin out a can and add homespun touches to its contents.

Last and not least, I've given plenty of people here a good belly-laugh. Part of the reason for writing up this diary is that I thought others may find my culinary adventures amusing too, whatever they think of my recipe ideas!

A lot has happened in just a hundred days. Visitors to Barra sometimes labour under the misapprehension that nothing changes here: that we're a traditional community caught in a time-warp, but looking back over the short time it took to do this challenge I can list some pretty major Barra-wide and domestic events:

Our bank was about to close then got an eleventh-hour reprieve
The supermarket freezers were out of order for a week in August
There were major disruptions to the ferries due to both weather and technical issues
The plane service suffered cancellations, mostly due to visibility problems: it turned back on occasion, giving passengers an unexpected three-hour flight in a tiny plane
We had all kinds of good – and very bad – weather
There were a number of power cuts, mostly brief but all potentially damaging
Power surges damaged sensitive equipment in the shops and elsewhere
Mobile phone signals were down for over a fortnight in October, affecting many people's livelihoods, including the taxi driver, who had to resort to WhatsApp
Our microwave died
Our laptop broke down

But… neither of us got ill, not once. And that's what we'd expect: we're annoyingly healthy now we're not full-time workers and more in control of our lives. This is a great place to live, and we enjoy every single day.

References and Helpful Information
Books:

- Bleaker House by Nell Stevens, Barnes and Noble, 2017
- The Frugal Cook by Fiona Beckett, Absolute Press, 2008
- A House by the Shore by Alison Johnson, 1986, Victor Gollancz.
- Cooking with Tinned Fish by Bart van Olphen, Pavilion, 2015
- The Last of Us by Rob Ewing, Harper Collins, April 2016.
- The Chickpea Cookbook, by Heather Thomas, Ebury Press, 2017.
- The Hungry Student vegetarian cookbook by Charlotte Pike, Quercus, 2013
- Linda McCartney's Home Cooking, Bloomsbury, 1989
- Every Day is a Holiday by George Mahood, Kindle edition, 2014
- The Art of Preserving All Kinds of Animal and Vegetable Substances for Several Years (1811) by Nicolas Appert, Kindle edition
- The French connection in the early history of canning by J C Graham, Journal of the Royal Society of Medicine, vol. 74, May 1981
- Thomas Jefferson's Garden Book, Unc Press for the TJ Foundation, 1999, Amazon

Videos:

- "the David Attenborough of engineering" explaining how and why cans are made as they are: https://www.youtube.com/watch?v=hUhisi2FBuw
- Appert, Napoleon and canning: https://www.youtube.com/watch?v=5jSXPK73pps
- Opening cans without an opener: https://www.youtube.com/watch?v=EE3vMNwj7FQ
- Ten ways to open cans without an opener: https://www.youtube.com/watch?v=acnRB_sEKtc
- Lead poisoning from early cans: https://www.historytoday.com/sheila-rowbotham/canned-food-sealed-icemens-fate
- weird foodstuffs in cans: https://www.youtube.com/watch?v=lX-1CexeTUc
- making a rose out of an aluminium can: https://www.youtube.com/watch?v=MuoG8rTKF60

Index by Canned Food Type
(followed by day-numbers of recipes)

Lychees 83
Mandarins 26
Mixed Bean Salad 8
Mixed Beans in Spicy Sauce 43
Mushrooms 88
New Potatoes 3,98
Organic vegetarian hotpot 60
Pâté 36
Pearl Barley 68
Peas, processed/marrowfat/garden
11,15,19,35,40,44,52,57,77,88,89,100
Pineapple Rings or Chunks 20,21,56,84
Pink Grapefruit 94
Pinto Beans 97
Prunes 14
Ratatouille 10,73
Red Kidney Beans 9,24,28,49
Refried Beans 30,71,97
Rice Pudding 16
Soup, any condensed variety 39
Soup, broccoli and stilton 92
Soup, broccoli, pea and pesto 59
Soup, chilli-lime with yams 76
Soup, condensed mushroom 23,70
Soup, cream of tomato 48
Soup, leek and potato 87
Soup, low-fat tomato and three bean 4
Soup, root vegetable and turmeric 54
Soup, thick vegetable 24
Spaghetti Rings 21
Sweet and Sour Sauce 81

Sweetcorn 22,49,75,77
Tofu 41
Tomato Passata 77,96,98
Tomato Puree 4,49,50
Tomatoes, Plum or Chopped
27,33,37,38,51,66,67,72,77,78,91
Vegan Balti 53
Vegetable Bolognese 45
Vegetable chilli 73,80

Recipe Index

Vegan Dishes

There are 52 vegan recipes below, assuming you use vegan margarine or stock, e.g. Marigold Bouillon, where called for. Many of the other meals could easily be made vegan by people with access to more shops and replacement ingredients, for example by replacing the ready-made puff pastry brand available here with Jus-Rol or making your own if you're not as lazy as I am. You could omit cheese in other recipes (or replace it with alternatives such as Sheese) and use non-dairy versions of custard, yogurt and rice pudding. The vegans I know tend to be flexible and resourceful anyway; I'm sure they could show me a thing or two! Everything I describe in this book is vegetarian apart from the one can of haggis I was given, which I donated to charity. No animals were harmed in the making of these dishes!

Soups (and Spinning out Soups)

I've learned to love my stick blender in the course of these weeks of experimentation. I've also got to the bottom of vegetable soup essentials: you start with an allium, such as red or white onion, leek or garlic, or a strongly-flavoured base vegetable such as celery or fennel, both of which are related to parsley. Then add the main vegetable which will give the soup its name, lesser quantities of any other veg. you're using, and the liquid to make it a soup, such as stock/broth/bouillon or yeast extract dissolved in water. I add the liquid from the can of veg. at the same time and rinse the last traces from the can with a little of the water. Once everything's cooked up and diluted down, adjust the flavour with herbs and spices to your personal taste. At this point you may want to blend all or part of the soup, to make it creamy and smooth or with a smooth base and visible vegetable pieces within that. It could of course just be a broth with tasty veg. chunks. If it's too thin, there's always the option to take out half a cupful of the soup and stir in a tablespoon of cornflour, then when it's well dissolved stir it gradually into the soup and bring just to the boil, stirring all the time, to thicken it up.

Finally, there's the topping or garnish to make each bowlful more attractive and satisfying: you could sprinkle on fresh or dried herbs, swirl in a denser liquid such as pesto, yogurt or soured cream, or top with grated cheese, toasted breadcrumbs, popcorn or a slice of French toast cut into small cubes while still hot and floated on the soup. I've described various ways to make a soup more of a meal in the recipes below.

Soups

Sweet Baking

Day 5: **APRICOT PONE CAKE**
Day 14: **PRUNE CAKE**
Day 32: **HOT TEACUP COCONUT PUDS**
Day 32: **COCONUT COOKIES**
Day 46: **FANTA CAKE**
Day 55: **EASY APPLE N' CUSTARD TARTLETS**
Day 57: **SWEET SURPRISE PEA CAKE**
Day 58: **CANNED CARROT CAKE**
Day 58: **LOW GI CANNED CARROT LOAF**
Day 66: **SWEET VEG CAKE**
Day 72: **SMASHIN' MASH-UP TRAYBAKE**
Day 74: **CIDER APPLE CAN LOAF**
Day 78: **TIN TOM FRUIT TART**
Day 82: **BORLOTTI BEAN CAKE**
Day 84: **EXCEEDINGLY GOOD FAKES**
Day 90: **CAN O' WORMS HALLOWE'EN CUPCAKES**
Day 94: **PINK GRAPEFRUIT CAN CANAPÉS**

Other Sweet Things

Day 16: **RICE PUD PANCAKES**
Day 20: **PINEAPPLE PUD**
Day 20: **PIÑA COLADA**
Day 62: **TEN MINUTE TASTY TABLET**
Day 65: **WHISKING GALORE CHICKPEA PAVLOVA**
Day 69: **WITCH'S EARWAX HALLOWE'EN CLAGGUM**

Savoury Baking

Day 1: **BEAN AND CHEESE BRIDIES**
Day 2: **LENTIL HERBY LOAF**
Day 8: **SPICY BEAN CUPS**
Day 10: **RATATOUILLE PIE**
Day 13: **BAKED BEAN MUFFINS**
Day 18: **BOOTSTRAP BOLOGNESE PIE**
Day 21: **SPAGHETTI HOOP PIZZA**
Day 22: **SWEETCORN CORNBREAD**
Day 42: **CHERRY TOM LAVISH LASAGNE**
Day 45: **CAN CANNELLONI**
Day 48: **DELICIOUS RED SOUP BREAD**
Day 49: **LOW CARB CAULI-BASED PIZZA**
Day 52: **HALLOUMI AND PEA PASTRY-FREE FLAN**
Day 54: **HEARTY HEART-HEALTHY SHEPHERD'S PIE**
Day 63: **BEANY BAGUETTE**
Day 71: **CAN EMPANADAS**
Day 73: **BUNNY CHOW CAN-STYLE**
Day 75: **CANNED MEALIE BREAD**
Day 77: **MEXI-CAN ENCHILADAS**
Day 80: **LAZY LATTICE PIE**
Day 80: **PASTRY NIBNOBS**
Day 92: **CRUMBLE GRATIN TOPPING FOR SOUP OR STEW**
Day 94: **PINK GRAPEFRUIT CAN CANAPÉS**
Day 94: **TEAR-AND-SHARE DABBY-DOUGHS**
Day 98: **LORD WOOL - TIN PIE**
Day 98: **BAKED BEAN LASAGNE**

Other Savoury Dishes

Day 6: **QUICK CAN CURRY**
Day 9: **SPANISH CAN-ISH TORTILLA**
Day 11: **BUTTER BEAN AND CIDER CASSEROLE**
Day 17: **"LES RESTES" SLOW COOKED FRENCH CASSEROLE IN WINE**
Day 23: **CAN-DO MUSHROOM STROGANOFF**
Day 24: **YOU MUST BE KIDNEY! CHEAT'S PASTA BAKE**
Day 25: **HEARTY ARTY LINGUINE**
Day 28: **ALRIGHT JACKFRUIT FAJITAS**
Day 35: **PEA PASTA**
Day 37: **VEGAN TACOS**
Day 39: **BEAN AND VEG TOASTY-TOP FAKE BAKE**
Day 40: **A RISOTTO LESS ORDINARY**
Day 41: **TASTY TOFU STIR FRY**
Day 50: **CANNELLINI BEANY TOAST**
Day 51: **SPICY LASAGNE IN A MUG FOR ONE**
Day 61: **CHEESILY-MADE BEAN BURGERS**
Day 67: **CHILLI NON CARNE PASTA**
Day 81: **SWEET AND SOUR CHOPSTICK KEBABS**
Day 85: **BESIDE A CIDER STROGANOFF**
Day 88: **UPMA**
Day 91: **STICKY SAUSAGE SPAGHETTI**
Day 93: **TIN TAGINE**
Day 97: **BURRITOS**
Day 99: **GALLO PINTO**
Day 100: **RAVIOLI CHEESY SKEWERS**

Snacks, Nibbles, Treats and Sides

Day 3: **SWIFT POTATO SALAD**

Day 7: **CHARLIE'S VEGAN MAYO**

Day 15: **PEA GUACAMOLE**

Day 19: **PEA CROQUETTES**

Day 20: **PIÑA COLADA**

Day 20: **PINEAPPLE PUD**

Day 21: **PINEAPPLE SALSA**

Day 26: **ORANGEY BEETROOT**

Day 29: **CRISP BEANSPROUT COLESLAW**

Day 30: **REFRIED BEAN DIP WITH HALLOUMI AND PEPPERS**

Day 36: **MELBA TOAST**

Day 38: **HOT TOMATO SAUCE**

Day 44: **CHAMPION BEAN CHAMP**

Day 47: **GREEN BEAN FRITTERS**

Day 49: **EASY BEAN DIP**

Day 50: **LEFTOVER BEAN HOTCAKES**

Day 53: **LOW CARB TASTY CAULIFLOWER RICE**

Day 55: **ROSANNE'S MIDDLE EASTERN TAHINI SALAD**

Day 56: **TAKEAWAY STYLE PINEAPPLE SWEET N' SOUR SAUCE**

Day 62: **TEN MINUTE TASTY TABLET**

Day 64: **SPANISH FRIED GARBANZOS**

Day 69: **WITCH'S EARWAX HALLOWE'EN CLAGGUM**

Day 69: **MAHOGANY**

Day 75: **SLAW UNTO ITSELF**

Day 77: **FLOUR TORTILLAS**

Day 79: **PAN CAN FARINATA**

Hacks, Hints and Bargainaceous Budget Ideas

Day 3: **SWIFT POTATO SALAD**

Day 7: **CHARLIE'S VEGAN MAYO**

Day 12: **THREE P'S PRONTO SOUP**

Day 15: **PEA GUACAMOLE**

Day 17: **"LES RESTES" SLOW COOKED FRENCH CASSEROLE IN WINE**

Day 24: **YOU MUST BE KIDNEY! CHEAT'S PASTA BAKE**

Day 25: **TIP FOR WARMING BOWLS AND PLATES**

Day 35: **PEA PASTA**

Day 36: **MELBA TOAST**

Day 39: **BEAN AND VEG TOASTY-TOP FAKE BAKE**

Day 40: **A RISOTTO LESS ORDINARY**

Day 46: **FANTA CAKE**

Day 48: **DELICIOUS RED SOUP BREAD**

Day 49: **EASY BEAN DIP**

Day 50: **LEFTOVER BEAN HOTCAKES**

Day 51: **TASTIER TINNED TOMATOES**

Day 51: **SPICY LASAGNE IN A MUG FOR ONE**

Day 53: **LOW CARB TASTY CAULIFLOWER RICE**

Day 56: **TAKEAWAY STYLE PINEAPPLE SWEET N' SOUR SAUCE**

Day 59: **DOUBLED-UP SOUP**

Day 60: **CHEAT'S HOTPOT COBBLER**

Day 61: **CHEESILY-MADE BEAN BURGERS**

Day 62: **TEN MINUTE TASTY TABLET**

Day 65: **WHISKING GALORE CHICKPEA PAVLOVA**

Lightning Source UK Ltd.
Milton Keynes UK
UKHW041815070319

338693UK00001B/190/P